CHARLES EDWARD STUART
AND THE JACOBITES

1745

CHARLES EDWARD STUART
AND THE JACOBITES

Edited by Robert C. Woosnam-Savage

EDINBURGH: HMSO

© Glasgow Museums 1995

First published 1995

British Library Cataloguing in Publication Data

A catalogue record for this book is available from the British Library

Exhibition: Bonnie Prince Charlie: Fact and Fiction

Art Gallery and Museum, Kelvingrove, Glasgow

2 June – 27 August 1995

Front cover picture:

The Royal Collection © Her Majesty The Queen

MORIER, David (*fl* 1705-70)

An Incident in the Rebellion of 1745

ISBN 0 11 495302 3

CONTENTS

FOREWORD

Julian Spalding
Director
Glasgow Museums

THIS publication gives an overview of the events of 1745–6 from a broad perspective and in so doing provides a more balanced picture than is usually found. The Hanoverian elements are considered as well as the Jacobite ones though, of course, the emphasis falls on the Jacobite story as it was, after all, 'Charlie's Year'.

Two hundred and fifty years after these events it might seem possible for sentiment to be put aside and the past to be looked at without either a blinkered or romantic gaze. The team of noted contributors assembled for this book makes an attempt at this. Whether they succeed or not is for the reader to decide. This range of up-to-date opinion on the various issues of the '45 will encourage further study of the period.

The production of this book and the accompanying exhibition involved much team work and I should like to thank the eight essayists who worked on the project, and especially my own colleagues in Glasgow Museums and at HMSO (Scotland) Alastair Fyfe Holmes, Liz Fergusson and George Bowie.

Ian G. Robertson
Director
National Army Museum

IT is a great pleasure for the National Army Museum to be so closely associated with Glasgow Museums and HMSO in the Special Exhibition which commemorates the 250th anniversary of Prince Charles Edward Stuart and the abortive Jacobite Rising of 1745–46.

As the editor and the eight contributors to this book reveal, the events of those long-ago 9 months of campaigning in Scotland and England, as well as the punitive military operations in the Highlands which followed the Battle of Culloden, were by turns stirring, heroic, brutal, futile and ultimately tragic. They also generated a rich and sometimes mysterious cultural heritage.

The controversies surrounding persons and events (in both camps) which began within hours of the final battle have not yet been stilled, and it is invigorating to see how recent scholarship can both stimulate the historical debate and rekindle our feelings of kinship and humanity – most of all with those innocent victims and hapless communities destroyed by dynastic ambition, civil war and imperial conquest. In passing, it is also gratifying to note among the roll of contributors two scholars with National Army Museum connections: Alan Guy, Assistant Director (Collections) and Dr Stephen Bull, who worked at the Museum from 1985 until l990, when he took up his present post at the County and Regimental Museum, Preston.

INTRODUCTION

Robert C. Woosnam-Savage

O N 16 April 1746 on Drummossie Moor, near Inverness, a battle was fought – Culloden. A battle won by the British army, a battle no British army regiment has amongst its honours. The regiments of the Government forces included the 'Royals' – The Royal Scots – a Scottish regiment. This was not simply England versus Scotland, 'the last match'; this was a civil war.

There is still much debate as to the significance of the subject of Jacobitism[1] but what surely cannot be denied is that after 250 years and the creation of a mountain of literature and an unlikely tourist icon, the '45 and 'Bonnie Prince Charlie' are still very much with us. This book is not the 'whole story' and was never intended to be. Eight essays by leading scholars in the field cover eight areas which combine to give a picture of the events and culture of the time, ranging from George II's army to Jacobite glass. Each essay is provided with extensive notes from which the interested reader may go further. The map, family tree and chronology are provided for quick reference to names, dates and places.

Bruce P. Lenman's opening chapter on *The Place of Prince Charles and the '45 in the Jacobite Tradition* provides a summary which goes some way to clarifying the distorted and simplified images that have been handed down, one for instance being that Charles' supporters were all Catholic. As Professor Lenman points out, comparatively speaking, there were not many Catholics around to support Charles. Much of his support came from other discontented parties, such as the Episcopalians and antiunionists.

The brief biography *Prince Charles Edward Stuart* by Rosalind K. Marshall gives us a sketch of the man behind the myth. Stubborn as a child, and stubborn as an adult, his charisma still managed to charm many (even against their better judgement, for example, in the case of Lochiel). Not surprisingly it is this charismatic young man who is now a permanent fixture of popular Scottish history and legend.

The structure and performance of Charles's Jacobite army is examined in the following chapter *'The Most Despicable Enemy That Are'* by Allan L. Carswell. The usual image of a 'rebellious mob' of volunteers (or conscripts) fighting for the cause is replaced by one of an organised, paid and trained army, one that marched all the way to Derby and then fought an orderly retreat back to Scotland, and ultimately Culloden.

Today we think of a tour of duty in the services as lasting months rather than up to 20 years or more. This rather salutary fact is just one of many in Alan Guy's survey of the Government army that faced the Jacobite forces. What comes across in *King George's Army, 1714–50* is not the stereotype of the beaten conscript only used to squarebashing but a professional who had already gained expertise in 'counter-insurgency tactics'. This goes some way to demolishing the theories of those who suggest that if Lord George Murray and the Jacobite army had taken to the hills and continued a 'small war' of attrition the possible outcome would have been different. Alan Guy also notes one terrible irony of the '45, it helped make the Scottish soldier an integral part of the British army and Empire – in all its theatres of actions.

Although Culloden was a defeat for Charles and the death knell of the Jacobite cause it should not be forgotten that it was the only battle the Jacobites actually lost. Under generals such as Lord George Murray, all previous engagements were Jacobite victories. Stephen Bull gives a concise account of the achievements – and disasters – of both sides in *Battles of the '45*.

The symbolic importance and power of the Stuarts and the '45 is discussed in Murray G. H. Pittock's essay *Jacobite Culture*. It illuminates the difference between the real aspirations of Charles in his contemporary culture (he was seen as the embodiment of mythical kingship) and how we view his aspirations today through the distorting lens of romanticism.

The mythologising of the '45, and ensuing confusion, is nowhere better represented than in Jacobite glass. Brian J. R. Blench examines these myths in *Symbols and Sentiment*. This chapter pulls together the work that has been produced regarding this subject, including the most recent. It raises a number of questions, including such basic ones as what is the significance of much Jacobite imagery.

The concluding chapter by Alan I. Macinnes, *The Aftermath of the '45*, is a powerful and highly charged account of what became of the Highlands immediately following the rebellion. It shows how this treatment paved the way for the later clearances. This is a contentious subject. It must not be forgotten that the Disarming Act of 1746 was only finally repealed in 1867.

These eight essays provide a basis for further reading and study. They prove that proper examination of the '45 is still worth pursuing; it is neither a frivolous exercise nor one that has been exhausted. To quote the contemporary Gaelic poet MacMhaigstir Alasdair, '...historians of the present time, seize the pen and paper; this is the special year...'[2]

Curator (Arms and Armour)
Department of History,
Glasgow Museums

Notes

1. See, for instance, C. Small, 'The Strong Command, The Weak Obey', *The '45 To Gather an Image Whole*, ed. L Scott-Moncrieff, Edinburgh, 1988, pp 179–95, J C D Clark, 'On Moving the Middle Ground. The Significance of Jacobitism in Historical Studies', *The Jacobite Challenge*, eds. E Cruickshanks and J Black, Edinburgh, 1988, pp 177–88 and introduction *The Jacobites, Britain and Europe 1688–1788*, D Szechi, Manchester, 1994, pp. 1–11, for debates on historiography.

2. Modern translation from W. Gillies, 'The Prince and the Gaels', *The '45 To Gather an Image Whole*, ed. L Scott-Moncrieff, Edinburgh, 1988, p 58.

LIST OF ILLUSTRATIONS

We are grateful to the following for permission to reproduce the illustrations used in this book.

Chapter 1

1. James Duke of York or Albany. National Galleries of Scotland
2. Reverse of medal celebrating the flight of James VII and II in 1688. Trustees of the National Museums of Scotland
3. Medal issued by supporters of William of Orange in 1696. Trustees of the National Museums of Scotland
4. The marriage of James Francis Stuart, the Old Pretender, and Clementina Sobieska in September 1719. By Masucci. Scottish National Portrait Gallery
5. Prince Charles Edward and his younger brother Henry. Trustees of the National Museums of Scotland
6. A Jacobite view of the abortive invasion of 1708. Trustees of the National Museums of Scotland
7. 'Bonnie Prince Charlie'. A contemporary portrait by the engraver Richard Cooper, produced in Edinburgh in 1745. National Library of Scotland
8. A leading Roman Catholic Jacobite of the '45, James 3rd Duke of Perth. Private Collection
9. Ivory snuff-mull in the form of a Highlander. It dates from *c*.1700-50. Trustees of the National Museums of Scotland
10. Fort George, Ardersier, Inverness-shire. Historic Scotland

Chapter 2

1. Prince James Francis Edward Stuart by an unknown artist. Scottish National Portrait Gallery
2. Princess Maria Clementina Sobieska by an unknown artist. Scottish National Portrait Gallery
3. Prince Charles Edward Stuart by an unknown artist. Scottish National Portrait Gallery

Chapter 3

Chapter 4

3. Silver tankard commemorating the battle of Culloden, 16 April 1746. Hallmarked London 1746–47, by Gabriel Sleath (d. 1756). Reproduced courtesy of the Director, National Army Museum, London

4. Lieutenant-Colonel (later Lieutenant-General) James Adolphus Oughton (1719–80) 37th Regiment of Foot. By George Knapton (1698–1778). Reproduced courtesy of the Director, National Army Museum, London

Chapter 5

1. Basket-hilted sword, with a hilt by Walter Allan of Stirling. Trustees of the National Museums of Scotland.

2. A fully armed, and traditionally clad, Highland soldier and corporal of the mid 18th century. Glasgow Museums

3. Plan of the battle of Culloden 16 April 1746. The Royal Collection © Her Majesty The Queen

4. The King's Colour of Barrel's Regiment, carried at Culloden. Trustees of the National Museums of Scotland

5. Laurie and Whittle's print of the battle of Culloden, published in London 1797. Trustees of the National Museums of Scotland

Chapter 6

1. 'Amor et Spes' Britannia medal, produced in protest against the Treaty of Aix-la-Chapelle (1748). Scottish National Portrait Gallery and the National Library of Scotland

2. 1750 Oak Society medal, minted in support of Charles Edward Stuart. Scottish National Portrait Gallery and the National Library of Scotland

3. 'The Agreable Contrast'. 1740s Jacobite print. Scottish National Portrait Gallery

4. Jacobite print depicting Charles Edward as Highland hero. Scottish National Portrait Gallery and the National Library of Scotland

5. Anti-Jacobite print of Charles Edward as 'Pied Piper' figure. Scottish National Portrait Gallery and the National Library of Scotland

6. Anti-Jacobite print of 'Betty Burke'. Scottish National Portrait Gallery

Chapter 7

1. The Erskine of Cardross II 'Amen' glass. Glasgow Museums

2. Enamel portrait glass. Trustees of the National Museums of Scotland

3. Enamel portrait glass. Glynn Vivian Art Gallery, Swansea.

4. Waterbowl engraved with seven-petalled rose and half-open bud on a stem with five leaves. On the reverse is a moth. Drambuie Collection

5. Wine glass engraved with six-petalled rose, half-open bud and five leaves. Drambuie Collection

6. Decanter engraved with eight-petalled rose, three quarter and half-open buds, seven leaves. Drambuie Collection

DVKE OF YORK

Chapter One

THE PLACE OF PRINCE CHARLES AND THE '45 IN THE JACOBITE TRADITION

Bruce P. Lenman

THE term 'Jacobite' was in use both in Scotland and England before 1689. It was used in late medieval Scotland as a synonym for a Dominican friar, from the Dominican hospice of St Jacques, in Latin *Sanctus Jacobus*, in Paris. In England, this adjective, formed from the latinised version of the personal name 'James', came to be used to describe anything pertaining to the reign of James VI of Scots and I of England and Ireland. The modern adjective for this era between 1603 and 1625 would be 'Jacobean'. However, when the political crises of 1688-9 saw James VII and II ousted from his English and Scottish thrones by his son-in-law, William of Orange, and his daughter, Mary, the term 'Jacobite' was conveniently to hand. It was used as early as 1689 by the English author Edmund Bohun in the title of his book *The History of the Disertion* ... in which he contrasted 'Williamites', who supported the Glorious Revolution which had toppled James, with 'Jacobites' who supported the deposed monarch. Similar usage can be found in Scotland about the same time.[1] This particular connotation for the word rapidly became universal, and it is normal to refer to the campaigns in Ireland between 1689 and 1691, which saw the expulsion of the luckless James II from his last kingdom, as the Jacobite War.

1. James Duke of York or Albany (as he was known in Scotland) before he became King James VII and II in 1685.

National Galleries of Scotland

Once James and the rest of his family were finally driven into exile, first at the palace of St Germain in France, and eventually in the Palazzo Muti in Rome, Jacobite activity could only assume the forms of propaganda, plotting, rebellion and invasion. Indeed, the whole point of Jacobite plotting was usually to try to organise a rebellion, preferably supported by an invasion by a major European power, hopefully France,

2. Reverse of medal gleefully celebrating the flight of James VII and II in 1688. Father Petre (James' Jesuit confessor) carries off the 'bogus' Prince of Wales to France in a French ship, offering him misplaced words of comfort as he does so.

the only western European power with the military and naval muscle capable, if focused on the task, of forcing the restoration of the exiled senior branch of the House of Stuart to its three thrones. In the event, despite decade after decade of relentless plotting, there were to be only three more Jacobite rebellions after the small rising in 1689-90 led by Viscount Dundee in Scotland. These were in 1715–16, 1719 and 1745–6. All three were primarily Scottish in their local basis. There was a small English rising in 1715, and the 1719 was entirely due to a small-scale Spanish invasion of north-west Scotland, but in terms of committed local support, Scotland was always the epicentre of the upheavals. Indeed, localisation of support was carried further, for within Scotland the Gaelic-speaking Highlands always produced the great bulk of the Jacobite armies. This last fact has fascinated historians, who have produced various explanations for it.

A view first advanced at length in the 1930s held that in the 28 years between the return of the Stuarts from their first exile in 1660 and the Glorious Revolution, Charles II and more especially James VII and II had shown themselves quite exceptionally sympathetic, patriarchal rulers in the Highlands, so that for the first time the inhabitants of that violent area felt a deep bond with Stuart kingship, a bond which survived the Revolution.[2] The trouble with this point of view is that, probed by serious scholarship, it emerges as an absurd reversal of fact. The Scottish Highlands after 1660 were not particularly violent. Serious crime appears to have been rarer in them than in the contemporary Lowlands. Highland chiefs and landowners were civilised men who preferred legal title to violent seizure. Clansmen were reluctant to fight for territory not inhabited by members of their own clan, and most of the physical disturbances which occurred were concentrated in the exceptional area of Lochaber where the claims of the only three clans habitually involved in disorders overlapped: the MacDonalds of Keppoch, the MacDonalds of Glencoe and the Camerons. The real destabiliser in the Highlands was an irresponsible and dictatorial Restoration Scottish monarchy which right up to the eve of the Revolution propagated a myth of Highland lawlessness to justify the cynical use of military force for purposes of political and personal advantage.[3]

It is, in fact, difficult to explain the longevity of Jacobitism in terms of the performance of the Stuart dynasty before 1688. In Charles I and James VII and II it produced two of the most incompetent and catastrophic exponents of personal monarchy in the 17th century, both marked by a recurring family trait: a pathological lack of interest in any point of view except their own. Arguably, the Scottish aristocracy and gentry performed a major national service in the years 1688–90 by preventing the politico-military crisis from escalating to the point where Scotland was plunged into the sort of blood-bath which the Marquis of Montrose had inflicted on it by his campaigns of 1644–6. This crisis-management was a profoundly pragmatic performance.[4] The political polarisation and ideological zeal which made subsequent Jacobite risings feasible developed quite soon after the Revolution. For example, the decision in 1690 to install a solely Presbyterian order in the Kirk by Law Established was forced on a reluctant William III by the intransigent Jacobitism of Bishop Rose of Edinburgh and his colleagues on the episcopal bench. The fact that William could not follow his original preference and keep bishops in the Kirk (because they were hostile), proved a priceless asset to Jacobitism.

A very large number of ministers would not accept the destruction of the polity of the Restoration kirk, which combined presbyteries and bishops, and their aristocratic patrons resented the attempts, frequently unavailing, of the government to oust these ministers from their parishes. Such ministers produced and preached the core doctrines of Scottish Jacobitism. These stressed the indefeasible hereditary right of the exiled Stuarts; the wrath of God at the national sin of the Revolution, and the need for restoration of Scotland's ancient dynasty as the only way to peace and order.[5] Bishop Rose was rapidly expelled from St Giles'

Cathedral, but he went on ministering to his flock in what is now Old St Paul's in Edinburgh. As the plaque on the wall of that kirk reminds us, members of its congregation were exceedingly active Jacobites in both the '15 and the '45. The reason why Glasgow displayed so little enthusiasm for Prince Charles in 1745–6, and indeed was treated by him as a hostile, conquered city when he occupied it in December and January 1745–6, was that it was so strongly Presbyterian.

Of course, there were other groups on whose support Charles could lean. Scottish Roman Catholics tended to be sympathetic to a Catholic dynasty. After Charles had touched on the southern part of the Outer Hebrides, and had been told to go back to France, he deliberately sailed to Arisaig, a Catholic pocket on the western seaboard of the mainland where he knew he could lurk in safety. The trouble was that Roman Catholics were few. Alexander Webster, in his remarkable demographic survey of Scotland which he produced in 1755 reckoned that out of a population of *c.*1,265,000, there were about 16,500 Catholics.[6] The figure is surely too low, but there is no doubt that before mass migration from Ireland in the 19th century, Scottish Catholicism existed in a few scattered pockets. There was a small one on the western side of the Borders. There was Arisaig. The biggest was the Enzie region in the north-east, protected by the Dukes of Gordon, but even they were

4

ambiguous conservatives rather than committed Catholic Jacobites. Bishop Hugh MacDonald, Roman Catholic Vicar Apostolic of the Highlands, was one of the first to hear of the landing of Prince Charles. He was not pleased and prophesied, correctly, that it would lead to disaster.[7]

Compared with this sort of realism, the mystical devotion to the House of Stuart which could still be found in Episcopalian circles was crucial in giving Charles a hard core of devoted supporters, some of them of real moral stature. It was said of the elderly Lord Pitsligo that when he rode into the Jacobite camp during the '45, men felt that Virtue and Religion had joined them. Religion alone has in Europe more often than not been a murderously divisive force. There was plenty of division, real and incipient, in the Jacobite ranks, from start to finish. Of the 'seven men of Moidart' who landed with Charles, four were Irish. Because the Irish aristocracy was overwhelmingly Protestant after 1690, and Jacobite risings simply did not happen without aristocratic, or at least gentry leadership, Irish Jacobitism was exilic. Some 12,000 Irish soldiers went into exile in France after the Treaty of Limerick of 1691 alone. Yet, even if there were exiled Irish with Charles in 1745, it has to be said there were not just four Irishmen at Moidart: there were four Irelands, for the men represented all the contradictions and rival religions and cultures of the island. Charles was one of the few things they could agree about.[8]

In the course of the campaigns in late 1745 and early 1746, relations between the Scots in the Jacobite leadership and the Irish in Prince Charles' entourage deteriorated disastrously. There were also plenty of divisions of language, religion and region among the leading Scots Jacobites, but they did contrive to pull together surprisingly well. Partly, this was due to the fact that Prince Charles was a different man from his dour and dictatorial grandfather James VII and II, and indeed from his worthy but deeply boring father, James Francis Edward Stuart, 'the Old Pretender'. Both were products of the baroque culture of the Counter-Reformation, passionately committed to their religious denomination as their central source of identity. Had Charles succeeded in 1745–6, his father would have abdicated. He did not want to live in London, surrounded by heretics.

Charles was very much a prince of the lighter rococo culture of the 18th century, a culture appalled in retrospect by the religious wars of the 17th century. He was well aware of the price his family had paid for its

religious obsessions, and between 1746 and 1766, when it was far too late, he flirted with Anglicanism. Scots Jacobites had been consciously trying to rise above denominational divisions for some time, using freemasons' lodges as one of their means of doing so. Though not popular with the papacy, freemasonry was countenanced by the great Roman Catholic monarchies, and many Scottish freemasons were Catholic and Jacobite. They formed networks of lodges in Continental Europe. Charles' one-time tutor, the Chevalier Michael Ramsay, had been prominent in this. The prince's secretary throughout the '45, and a very good secretary he was, John Murray of Broughton, had joined one of these lodges in Rome in 1737.[9] He was himself an Episcopalian, but one of the themes of contemporary freemasonry was that religion was too important to be left to priests, and that true religion should unite, not divide, men. Universalism of this kind was very much an élite view. Murray of Broughton was captured in 1746 and turned King's Evidence against Lord Lovat, who was executed. Nevertheless, in his Jacobite phase, Broughton helps to demonstrate, not that the '45 was a freemasons' plot, but that the lay élite of Scottish Jacobitism was consciously trying, with some success, to rise above the intolerance and venom of sectarianism.

None of this would have enabled Charles to take over Scotland as easily as he did — with a quarter of an hour of fighting at Prestonpans after he

4. The marriage of James Francis Edward Stuart, the Old Pretender, and Clementina Sobieska in September 1719. The wedding took place at midnight.
Its sole achievement before it went sour was the securing of a Jacobite succession by the birth of Prince Charles and his brother Henry. Painting by Masucci.

Scottish National Portrait Gallery

had occupied Edinburgh — had not other factors inclined some Presbyterians to co-operate with and the great bulk of them to acquiesce in the activities of the Jacobite minority. Two factors were critical. They overlapped but were not identical. One was disillusionment with the way post-Revolution government continued all the worst features of late Stuart absolutism. We now know that the massacre of Glencoe of 1692 was a last-minute retargetting of a punitive strike originally aimed at the MacDonells of Glengarry.[10] Nevertheless, it represented a continuation of the style and methods of the regime of James VII: secretive, irresponsible and given to confusing ruthlessness with efficiency.

Nor did the passage of time lead to more acceptable government. As early as the 1640s during the War of the Three Kingdoms, it had become apparent just how tyrannical a minority-based majority in the Westminster House of Commons could be, as it exploited the dogma of the sovereignty of parliament. After the accession of the House of Hanover in the person of George I in 1714, Great Britain experienced a virtual coup by the Whig party, almost certainly a minority in the political nation. It smashed the rival Tory party and cemented itself into power, never more so than under Prime Minister Sir Robert Walpole in the 1720s and 1730s. With a German king, a professional army and the unbridled claims which parliamentary sovereignty gave them over all

5. The alternative to the Whig ascendancy: The last of the Royal Stuarts: Prince Charles Edward and his younger brother Henry.

Trustees of the National Museums of Scotland

subordinate bodies, the Whigs ran a one-party state of a notably corrupt kind whose power in Scotland was usually mediated through the ascendant Scots Whig faction, the Argathelians or followers of the Campbell Dukes of Argyll. Those who could not climb on the Campbell bandwagon, and there were many, for loaves and fishes were in limited supply, could be driven to despair, while Scotland's venal MPs and contemptibly servile 'representative' peers were held in general disdain.[11] Charles could mine deep-seated discontents in 1745.

6. *A Jacobite view of the abortive invasion of 1708 shows the three British realms appealing for the return of their rightful heir. 'Reddite' means return.*

He also clearly drew on passionate Scottish nationalism. Scots accepted that they had to have a relationship with England. What they resented was being denied any serious say in the form of that relationship. Modern scholarship has demonstrated beyond question that the Act of Union of 1707 was not a negotiated package but a political job pushed through the old Scots parliament by the executive by the crude but effective device of buying the leader of the opposition, the Duke of Hamilton.[12] The London politicians were lucky not to have to pay a heavy price for so offending the bulk of Scottish opinion. In 1708, there was a Franco-Jacobite invasion plan suggested originally by the devious Simon Fraser, Lord Lovat, then in exile in France. It involved transporting James Francis Edward Stuart, the twenty-year-old 'Old Pretender', with a force of French infantry, to the Firth of Forth on a squadron of swift privateer ships, to head a Jacobite rising. The Whig commander-in-chief in North Britain later said he lacked troops to resist a rising, which would then have occupied the northern English coalfields, the source of London's energy supply, to force the English to the negotiating table. The scheme was wrecked only by the incompetence of the French admiral,[13] but there was plenty of anti-Union sentiment around in 1715 and 1745.

It is true that only in the Highlands was it still possible to raise armed men in large numbers, but the idea that Jacobite risings were essentially an attempt to defend an archaic Celtic culture is belied by the fact that many Jacobite leaders were aggressive, business-oriented modernisers.[14] That an understandably enraged and paranoid Westminster government set out to smash Celtic culture and the clans after Culloden should not obscure the strictly contemporary reasons for the '45. Above all, its timing was determined by international affairs. After a long period of friendly co-existence, Anglo-French relations had deteriorated to the point of open war by 1744, when Prince Charles had been brought to France to act as the political figurehead for a massive French invasion of southern England. Alas for his hopes, by 1745 the French had cancelled the project. What Charles was trying to do with his private-enterprise expedition to Scotland in the late summer of 1745 was to raise a successful enough rising, on the back of Scottish discontent, to persuade the French to reactivate their invasion of England option. Charles knew that this was probably his last chance.[15]

7. 'Bonnie Prince Charlie'. A contemporary portrait by the engraver Richard Cooper produced in Edinburgh in 1745. This was in fact a 'wanted' poster, the caption stating 'A likeness notwithstanding the Disguise that any Person who Secures the Son of the Pretender is Intitled to a Reward of 30.000£'.

National Library of Scotland

8. A leading Roman Catholic Jacobite of the '45, James 3rd Duke of Perth.

Private Collection

His success in persuading men of substance to join him hinged on three statements. One was true: Scotland was absurdly ill-defended by Westminster. The other two were dangerous lies. Charles said the French king had already agreed to send substantial aid. He also said the English Tories were pledged to rise for him. After his seizure of Scotland, the bulk of his council did not really want to invade England.

Charles forced that policy through by one vote. Because he had no serious cavalry, Charles could invade in winter without waiting for spring grass for the horses. What he never grasped was that his Scottish supporters did not want to impose a king on the English whom the English did not want. Most of the Scots chiefs and officers regarded the invasion as a reconnaissance in force to test opinion. By the time the Jacobite army reached Derby, only 200 unemployed from Manchester had joined them; the French had obviously not been committed to send immediate aid; and Charles had to admit he did not have a single letter from an English Tory. Even his closest Roman Catholic associates were appalled. Charles' contact with reality was minimal. Lord George Murray had commanded the army while Charles burbled on about how he should dress when he entered London in triumph and whether on horse or foot. When his principal supporters in effect challenged him as an irresponsible liar, he banged his head against walls and screamed abuse at them.[16]

Lord George's retreat to Scotland in the face of three hostile armies with formidable cavalry was brilliant. The delaying action at Clifton and the Battle of Falkirk were remarkable tactical achievements, but disaster

9. One of the few contemporary images of an armed clansman, this ivory snuff-mull is in the form of a Highlander. It dates from c.1700-50.

Trustees of the National Museums of Scotland

finally caught up with Charles in April 1746 in the first battle where he truly commanded, on the totally unsuitable site of Culloden or Drummossie Moor. He never had much of a chance of success. The idea that the Tory party was Jacobite was just not true. There was a Jacobite minority of between 43 and 57 MPs in the parliamentary Tory party c.1714.[17] In 1745, Tory MPs and peers positively fell over themselves to go to Westminster to pay homage to George II, despite a proclamation from Charles denouncing attendance at the 'Elector of Hanover's' parliament as treason to his father.[18] As for the longed-for French invasion, the Royal Navy had the key French ports well blockaded and indeed by 1746 was forming a tight enough naval screen around Scotland to cut off crucial French supplies of money in such a way

10. Fort George, Ardersier, Inverness-shire

This mighty structure (begun 1748 completed 1769) was built after the '45 to cope with the next Jacobite rising. It never came.

Historic Scotland

as to force Charles to fight at Culloden before his army started to disintegrate due to lack of funds.[19] There was not the slightest prospect of a Jacobite rising in Ireland, where the Viceroy, Lord Chesterfield, was cynically relaxed throughout the '45.[20] In England, there was no support for Charles, however much apathy there might be towards the cause of the Westminster government. The only constructive use of Charles' initial coup, and even that would have been difficult, would have been to try to hang on and wear England down into acknowledging Scottish independence while England was mired in a losing war with France, but then there was no case for invading England.

Charles was lucky. His combination of vigour and stubbornness, plus support from long-standing Scottish loyalties, aided by a unique international situation, enabled him to carve out a permanent niche in romantic history in a year. Even if his final escape was colluded at by the Whig General Campbell,[21] his period as a fugitive enhanced his image to the point where people forget that he would probably have been a disastrous monarch. Autocratic, immature, totally self-centred, and with no political realism in him, he was lucky in his Scotland. As Lord George Murray in effect told him in a famous and very angry letter written immediately after Culloden: Scotland was less lucky in him.

Bibliography

1. Edmund Bohun, *The History of the Disertion, or an Account of all the Publick Affairs in England, from the beginning of September 1688 to the Twelth of February following...* London, 1689; *A Dictionary of the Older Scottish Tongue*, eds Sir William Craigie and A.J. Aitken, University of Chicago Press, Chicago, and Oxford University Press, London, 1937, Vol III, p. 334; and *The Oxford English Dictionary*, 2nd. edn., eds. J.A. Simpson and E.S.C. Weiner, Clarendon Press, Oxford, 1989, Vol. VIII, p. 174.

2. Audrey Cunningham, *The Loyal Clans*, Cambridge University Press, Cambridge, 1932, esp. ch. IX, 'The Divine Right of Kings'.

3. Allan I. Macinnes, 'Repression and Conciliation: The Highland Dimension 1660-1688', *The Scottish Historical Review*, LXV, 1986, pp. 167-95.

4. Bruce P Lenman, 'The Poverty of Political Theory in the Scottish Revolution of 1688-90', in *The Revolution of 1688-89: Changing Perspectives*, ed. Lois G. Schwoerer, Cambridge University Press, Cambridge, 1992, pp. 244-59.

5. Bruce P Lenman, 'The Scottish Episcopal Clergy and the Ideology of Jacobitism', in *Ideology and Conspiracy: Aspects of Jacobitism, 1689-1759*, ed. Eveline Cruickshanks, John Donald, Edinburgh, 1982, pp. 36-48.

6. Alexander Webster, 'An Account of the Number of People in Scotland in the Year 1755', in *Scottish Population Statistics*, ed. James G. Kyd, Scottish Historical Society, 3rd series, vol. XLIV, misnumbered on half title p. XLIII, Edinburgh, 1952, p. 77.

7. Bruce P Lenman, *The Jacobite Clans of the Great Glen 1650-1784*, Methuen, London, 1984, p. 149.

8. Owen Dudley Edwards, 'The Long Shadows: A View of Ireland and the '45' in *The '45: To Gather an Image Whole*, ed. Lesley Scott-Moncrieff, The Mercat Press, Edinburgh, 1988, pp. 73-89.

9. vide, *Memorials of John Murray of Broughton*, ed. Robert Fitzroy Bell, Scottish History Society, Vol. XXVII, Edinburgh, 1898, Intro. pp. x-xi.

10. Paul Hopkins, *Glencoe and the End of the Highland War*, John Donald, Edinburgh, 1986.

11. Bruce P. Lenman, 'A Client Society: Scotland between the '15 and the '45', in *Britain in the Age of Walpole*, ed. Jeremy Black, Macmillan, London, 1984, pp. 69-93.

12. P.H. Scott, *1707: The Union of Scotland and England*, Chambers, in association with the Saltire Society, Edinburgh, 1979.

13. John S. Gibson, *Playing the Scottish Card: The Franco-Jacobite Invasion of 1708*, Edinburgh University Press, Edinburgh, 1988.

14. Bruce P. Lenman, *The Jacobite Risings in Britain 1689-1746*, Eyre Methuen, London, 1980.

15. The best summary of the extensive literature on this is now Daniel Szechi, *The Jacobites: Britain and Europe 1688-1788*, Manchester University Press, Manchester, 1994, chap. 4.

16. Rosalind K. Marshall, *Bonnie Prince Charlie*, HMSO, Edinburgh, 1988, pp. 117-24.

17. D. Szechi, *Jacobitism and Tory Politics 1710-14*, John Donald, Edinburgh, 1984.

18. William A. Speck, *The Butcher: The Duke of Cumberland and the Suppression of the '45*, Basil Blackwell, Oxford, 1981, pp. 63-4.

19. John S. Gibson, *Ships of the '45*, Hutchinson, London, 1967.

20. Bruce P. Lenman, 'Scotland and Ireland 1742-1789' in *British Politics and Society from Walpole to Pitt 1742-1789*, ed. Jeremy Black, Macmillan, London, 1990, pp. 81-7.

21. John S. Gibson, *Lochiel of the '45*, Edinburgh University Press, Edinburgh, 1994, p. 154.

Chapter Two

PRINCE CHARLES EDWARD STUART

Rosalind K. Marshall

AT one time 'Bonnie Prince Charlie' was the undisputed hero of folk tale and song: the dashing young man who suddenly appeared in Scotland to lead the brave Highlanders against Hanoverian oppression, suffered overwhelming defeat at Culloden and, after dreadful privation and many hair-raising escapes, vanished to the Continent, never to be seen again. Scholars might point to the documentary detail of his life, but such was the largely accepted view until the late 20th century, when people suddenly became disillusioned with Charles, blaming him for failure, focusing on his more unfortunate personal characteristics, emphasising his rashness and his alcoholism, and somehow attributing to him many of the perceived ills of society in contemporary Scotland. Both these views distort by exaggeration, but the truth, in so far as we can know it, is no less colourful.

Born in Rome on 21 December 1720, at his father's exiled court, this 'brave, lusty boy' aroused from the beginning impossibly high expectations. Prince James Francis Edward, 'the Old Pretender', had long since given up any active attempt to win back the throne of Britain for himself. Instead, he sat in the Palazzo Muti writing endless letters to his supporters throughout western Europe, weighed down by his sense of responsibility to them and his knowledge that those who shared his penurious exile had given up everything for his cause. Persuaded at last to marry, he took as his wife a vivacious young Polish princess half his age and completely different from him in nature. Where he was solemn and reserved, Clementina Sobieska was volatile, impetuous and outging.

1. Prince James Francis Edward Stuart by an unknown artist.

Scottish National Portrait Gallery

Their incompatibility all too soon became obvious to their courtiers, but when their first son was born, there was unalloyed rejoicing. Guns boomed out from the Castle Saint Angelo, fireworks exploded, people danced in the streets and some ardent Jacobites in near-blasphemous fashion claimed to have discovered a new star in the night sky. The tribulations of the past were swept away as they told each other in happy confidence that this new prince, Charles Edward Louis John Casimir Silvester Xavier Maria, would one day reclaim his inheritance and restore them all to their proper place in British society.[1]

Clementina was charmed with her large, handsome son. James's pleasure was, characteristically, overshadowed by anxiety as he contemplated the difficulties of moulding his wearingly noisy, wilful infant into the perfect Prince of Wales. Worse still, he had discovered that beneath his wife's pretty effervescence lay an implacable obstinacy and a fierce temper. Soon they were quarrelling bitterly over the baby's upbringing and Charles's first years were spent in an atmosphere of uninhibited family conflict, albeit he himself was the centre of the entire household's adoring attention.

When he was five, his brother Henry Benedict was born but, after a particularly spectacular quarrel with her husband, Clementina departed to a convent, where she remained for many months, emerging a changed woman. Ethereal, devoted to religion, spending long hours nursing the

poor and sick of Rome, she existed on the periphery of her family's life, treated by her husband and sons with a kind of respectful awe. Long subject to eating problems, she ruined her health by severe fasting, suffered from asthma, and died when Charles was twelve. In spite of past difficulties, James and his sons were deeply upset.

The younger boy, Henry, was like his father in nature, quiet and scholarly. He was James's favourite. Boisterous

18

5. Prince Henry Benedict Stuart in 1732, by Antonio David

Scottish National Portrait Gallery

Charles had a superabundance of energy, adored outdoor sports of all kinds but had little patience for sitting at his books. James found him childish and immature for his age, and when one of the courtiers reproached him for being too strict with the boy, he replied wearily, "There is no question of crushing the Prince's spirit and no danger of its being crushed, for he is mightily thoughtless and takes nothing much to heart."

Be that as it might, Charles was growing up with a desperate desire to please his demanding parent, and a conviction that there was only one way to do so. He had always loved romantic tales of chivalry, and by the time he was in his teens he saw himself as a latter-day medieval knight, riding to the rescue of the Stuart family fortunes. Hunting and shooting were not merely absorbing leisure pursuits. They were training for the battlefield. He pored over military manuals, plans of fortifications and model forts, all his thoughts and energies directed to the day when he would be asked to lead an invasion of Britain.[2]

When he was twenty-two, the summons came. France and Britain were at war, the French army had been defeated at Dettingen and Louis XV was seeking revenge. His forces would invade England and depose the Hanoverian George II. Charles would lead the army, and when victory was won, he would rule as Regent for his father, King James III.

At the end of December 1743, Charles left Rome, travelling incognito to Paris and on to Dunkirk, where the fleet was assembling. Field Marshal Saxe, France's leading military commander, wanted no part in the invasion, and when a sudden storm seriously damaged the transport vessels and the small accompanying fleet, the Government gladly cancelled the project. The Prince was bitterly disappointed, but he was not to be deterred. It was impossible to set off for England without an army of invasion, but he would sail for Scotland, where he had been told that numerous supporters would welcome him.

The following June, he and a little group of companions set sail from St Nazaire aboard the *Du Teillay* [3] to disembark, on 23 July, in pouring rain on the island of Eriskay. Convinced that the British were longing for him to liberate them from the Hanoverian oppressor, he was astonished when first one clan chief and then another told him to go home. Determined not to retreat, he sailed to the mainland. There, the initially sceptical Donald Cameron of Lochiel was won over by Charles's sheer force of personality, and with Lochiel's promise of support, other chiefs began to come in too. On 19 August 1745 Charles raised his father's standard at Glenfinnan. The Rising had begun.

While the Government despatched a small army under Sir John Cope to intercept him, he and his men marched down through the Pass of Corrieyairack, along General Wade's roads to Blair Atholl, on to Dunkeld, Perth, Linlithgow and so to Edinburgh. One of his Lieutenants-General was the highly experienced Lord George Murray. Under his command, the Jacobites took Scotland's capital without shedding a drop of blood and the Prince installed himself in the Palace of Holyroodhouse.

Far from throwing balls, dancing and flirting with the Edinburgh ladies as tradition asserts, Charles devoted all his attention to military matters, for he was looking forward eagerly to an encounter with the Government forces. The two armies finally met at Prestonpans on 21 September and fears about the Highlanders' performance in the face of

6. Prince Charles Edward Stuart in 1745, engraved by Sir Robert Strange

Scottish National Portrait Gallery

AVERSO MISSUS
SUCCURRERE SECLO

the Government redcoats melted away. The Jacobites triumphed. Routed, Cope fled to Berwick, yet in the aftermath of victory, Charles's officers were surprised to find him in sombre mood. London, not Edinburgh, was the real objective, he said, and they must now conquer the south. The clan chiefs were dismayed. They had done what they had come to do, and now they wanted to go home. Charles remained adamant, and reluctantly they agreed to follow him south.[4]

Marching at the head of his army, in highland dress, he led his men across the River Esk into England, only to discover that the support he had so confidently anticipated was not forthcoming.[5] Moreover, George II dispatched not just one Government army under the ageing General Wade but a second force under his own favourite son, the young and energetic Duke of Cumberland. By the time the Jacobites reached Derby, Lord George Murray knew that they must turn back or suffer complete defeat.

The Prince was appalled, and for once his charm and his obstinacy had no effect. The members of his council of war were united in their determination to turn back. On Black Friday, 6 December 1745, Charles rode northwards out of the town with them, in a mood of savage despair, yet such was his resilience that by the time they re-entered Manchester, he seemed in the best of spirits, having convinced himself that this was merely a strategic withdrawal, not a retreat.

They crossed the Border once more on the Prince's twenty-fifth birthday, and marched to Glasgow. Wade had now been replaced and his army was commanded by General Henry Hawley. When he heard that Hawley had arrived in the east of Scotland, Charles moved to meet him. Pausing at Bannockburn House, near Stirling, he made the acquaintance of the owner's niece, Clementina Walkinshaw, who soon became his mistress, but this interlude did nothing to hinder his resolve. The two forces met at Falkirk. After a brief battle in appalling weather, the Jacobites were once more victorious, but many of the Highlanders thought in the confusion that they had been defeated and fled north. Lord George Murray recommended that the rest follow. The winter could be spent in the Highlands, gathering the clansmen together again, and in the spring they could advance south once more.

They marched through snow and rain, to Inverness, pursued by the Duke of Cumberland. The final encounter took place at Culloden, on 16

April 1746. The exhausted Jacobites were completely outnumbered. The Government cannon cut great swathes through their ranks, and the surviving clansmen stumbled forward to fall beneath a hail of musket fire or die on the redcoats' bayonets. The Prince watched the slaughter from a slope behind his second line, too shocked to move, said some, while others claimed that he had to be held back from plunging down to rally his men. In the end, one of his Irish friends took his horse's bridle and led him from the field.[6]

Even his sternest critics agree that in the ensuing months the Prince's courage and good humour were impeccable in conditions of extreme danger and discomfort.[7] After a half-hearted attempt to rally the clansmen at Fort Augustus, he and a little band of supporters fled to Glengarry and on to Arisaig. Escape to France seemed the only possibility if Charles were to survive, but no French vessel could yet slip past the British men-of-war patrolling the west coast. He was forced to travel on to Benbecula, sheltering in a series of wretched huts and bothies, his clothes soaking, his shoes disintegrating, his feet bleeding and his limbs numb with cold. His companions never heard him complain, and he supped his oatmeal with a shell as if it were the most tasty dish concocted by his father's cooks in Rome. Even when he suffered from dysentery, his patience and his self control amazed everyone. It may well be that the brandy he took in large quantities to settle his stomach plunged him into the alcoholism which plagued him for the rest of his life.

The best known episode of his Hebridean wanderings, his rescue by Flora Macdonald, has been romanticised. Flora never was his mistress, and although she was persuaded to take him over the sea to Skye, disguised as her maidservant Betty Burke, the part she played in his preservation was relatively slight. Neil MacEachain, a tutor in Clanranald's family who acted as his guide, did far more, and not one single Highlander betrayed him, despite of the price of £30,000 on his head. On 19 September 1746 he boarded a French vessel, *Le Prince de Conti*, and that same evening sailed for France.[8]

He lived for nearly forty-two more years. Welcomed back as a hero by the French people, who had believed him dead, he was obsessed with the desire to win Louis XV's support so that he could fight the Scottish campaign all over again.[9] He could not accept that there could be no second invasion. Seeking consolation with his pretty young married cousin, Louise, Duchesse de Montbazon, he fathered her son, Charles, who died six months later. By that time he taken as his mistress Marie Anne Louise Jablonowska, Princesse de Talmont, at forty-seven one of the leading courtesans of the day. Their relationship ended when Louis XV obeyed the terms of the Treaty of Aix-la-Chapelle and banished Charles from his territories.

7. Prince Charles Edward Stuart by Maurice Quentin de la Tour

Scottish National Portrait Gallery

There then ensued a lengthy period of concealment, long years of wandering through France, Switzerland, Germany and the Low Countries, under a series of assumed names and usually in disguise.[10] The Prince spent much of his time drinking heavily and planning abortive returns to Britain. It may well have been some of his more realistic supporters who persuaded Clementina Walkinshaw to join him, hoping that she would prove a distraction. She bore him a daughter, Charlotte, and they lived together in Ghent as man and wife until, unable to endure his drinking and ill-usage, Clementina took the little girl and fled to a convent.

In 1760, George II died and was succeeded peacefully by his grandson George III. Two years later, James Francis Edward suffered a stroke. He lingered on until 1 January 1766. Summoned by his brother Henry, now Cardinal York, Charles arrived in Rome too late to see his father, but he decided to remain there. Settling in the Palazzo Muti, he went shooting, listened to music, played the French horn and still managed to charm visitors. In 1771 his new way of life was disturbed when Louis XV, eager to annoy the British, offered him a lavish pension if he would marry and produce an heir. Charles thereupon dispatched to Germany an emissary, who came back with Louise of Stolberg, almost twenty, with dazzling fair skin, golden hair and dark eyes. Daughter of an impoverished widow, she was, in her eagerness to find a wealthy husband, prepared to overlook her bridegroom's less pleasing characteristics, or so she thought.

Intelligent and something of a bluestocking, she soon found her new life intolerable. Her husband's once splendid constitution had been ruined by drink. He was deaf, had asthma, dropsy and continual sickness. They moved to Florence, Louise gathered around herself a little circle of literary and artistic friends, and took as her lover Count Vittorio Alfieri, a romantic young poet. Finally, she ran away with him.

10. Charlotte, Duchess of Albany, by Hugh Douglas-Hamilton

Scottish National Portrait Gallery

The Prince's pride was hurt, but he found consolation. Charlotte, his daughter by Clementina Walkinshaw, came into his life again in 1784. By now the mistress of Cardinal Rohan and mother of his son and two daughters, she was desperate to provide for their future. Hoping to benefit financially, she joined her father in Florence. Delighted, he created her Duchess of Albany, bestowed the Order of the Thistle on her, took her about, showed her off and made her life a misery with his incessant demands, his possessiveness and his sudden rages.

Charles and she moved to Rome the following autumn, settling down in the Palazzo Muti. Sometimes, the Prince would listen with tears in his eyes as his piper played 'Lochaber No More'. Once, when an English visitor questioned him about the sufferings of the Jacobites after Culloden, he fainted. Rash he had been, obstinate and self absorbed, but he was a tragic figure, nevertheless. Unable to accept failure, he had spent more than forty years longing for the unattainable, his undoubted qualities of courage, grace and endurance sunk in a quagmire of guilt, inadequacy and lost self esteem.

Not long after his sixty-seventh birthday he suffered a stroke and on 21 January 1788 he died. He and his brother now lie with their father in St Peter's, beneath a handsome marble monument by Canova. It was erected at the instigation of the future George IV, some years after the death of Cardinal York. The Stuarts by then posed no further threat to the British throne. The savage realities of his life forgotten, 'Bonnie Prince Charlie' could safely be celebrated as one of the most romantic figures in Scotland's legendary past.

Bibliography

1. Biographies of James Francis Edward include Bryan Bevan, *King James the Third of England*, London, 1967; A and H Tayler, *The Old Chevalier*, London, 1934; and Peggy Miller, *James*, London, 1971. The events leading up to his marriage are detailed in John T Gilbert, ed., *Narratives of the Detention, Liberation and Marriage of Maria Clementina Stuart*, Irish University Press, 1970. H Tayler, gives background detail in *The Jacobite Court in Rome*, Scottish History Society, 1938. Contemporary descriptions of Prince Charles Edward's birth are to be found in *Diario Ordinario* no 54, 4 January 1721 and Scottish Record Office, Moray of Abercairney Muniments, GD24/1/487A.

2. The many biographies of Prince Charles Edward which describe the events of 1743-6 include Andrew Lang, *Prince Charles Edward Stuart*, London, 1900; Winifred Duke, *Prince Charles Edward and the '45*, London, 1939; Margaret Forster, *The Rash Adventurer*, London, 1973; David Daiches, *Charles Edward Stuart*, London, 1973, Rosalind K Marshall, *Bonnie Prince Charlie*, Edinburgh, 1988; Fitzroy Maclean, *Bonnie Prince Charlie*, London, 1988 and F J McLynn, *Charles Edward Stuart*, London, 1988.

3. W B Blaikie, ed., *Origins of the 'Forty Five*, Scottish History Society, 1975; *ibid. Itinerary of Prince Charles Edward Stuart*, Scottish History Society, 1897; Robert Chambers, *History of the Rebellion in Scotland in 1745-6*, i and ii Edinburgh, 1827; A and H Tayler, *1745 and After*, London, 1938; John Home, *The History of the Rebellion in the Year 1745*, London, 1802, Bruce P Lenman, *Jacobite Risings in Britain 1689-1748*, London, 1980; A J Youngson, *The Prince and the Pretender*, London, 1985; F J McLynn, *France and the Jacobite Rising of 1745*, Edinburgh, 1981; ed. Alastair Livingstone of Bachuil, *et al.*, *Muster Rolls of Prince Charles Edward Stuart's Army 1745-46*, Aberdeen, 1984 Evan Charteris, ed., *A Short Account of the Affairs of Scotland in the Years 1744, 1745, 1746*, Edinburgh, 1907.

4. Contemporary accounts of the campaign include Robert Chambers, *Jacobite Memoirs of 1745*, Edinburgh, 1834; Lord David Elcho, *A Short Account of the Affairs of Scotland*, ed. Evan Charteris, London, 1907; Chevalier de Johnstone, *Memoirs of the Rebellion*, London, 1820. See also K Tomasson, *The Jacobite General* (Lord George Murray), London, 1958; and Winifred Duke, *Lord George Murray and the '45*, London, 1938.

5. F J McLynn, *The Jacobite Army in England 1745,* Edinburgh, 1983.

6. K Thomson and F Buist, *Battles of the '45,* London, 1962; John Prebble, *Culloden,* London, 1961; John S Gibson, *Ships of the '45 :The Rescue of the Young Pretender,* London, 1967; ed. B G Seton, and J G Arnot, *The Prisoners of the '45,* Scottish History Society, 1928; Robert Forbes, *Lyon in Mourning,* i,ii,iii ed. Henry Paton, Scottish History Society, 1859; W A Speck, *The Butcher,* Oxford, 1981.

7. John Selby, *Over the Sea to Skye,* London, 1973; Alasdair Maclean, and John S Gibson, *Summer Hunting a Prince,* Stornoway, 1992.

8. The most recent biography of Flora MacDonald is by Hugh Douglas, *Flora Macdonald,* London, 1993.

9. L L Bongie, *The Love of a Prince,* Vancouver, 1986; C L Berry, *The Young Pretender's Mistress,* London, 1977.

10. Andrew Lang, *Pickle the Spy,* London, 1897; Henrietta Tayler, *Prince Charlie's Daughter,* London, 1950; Brian Fothergill, *The Cardinal King,* London, 1958.

Chapter Three

'THE MOST DESPICABLE ENEMY THAT ARE' – THE JACOBITE ARMY OF THE '45

Allan L. Carswell

THIS damning condemnation was written in January 1746 by Lieutenant General Henry Hawley, a British Army officer and a worried man. It was his parting shot in a special order issued prior to the Battle of Falkirk, which he hoped would dispel some of the rumours of Highland invincibility and ferocity that were eroding the already doubtful morale of his command.[1] His method was to explain how strict discipline and firepower, the bedrock of the British Army, would easily triumph over the despised Highlanders. When it came to the test, a few days later in the midst of a snow storm, his counsel went unheeded. As had happened at Prestonpans, a force of regular British troops was routed by the Jacobite Army. Even for a man whose uncomplicated attitude to military discipline had earned him the nickname of 'hangman', Hawley was an intemperate and brutal man. However, his prejudice against what he regarded as the 'arrant scum' who made up the bulk of the Jacobite Army and his disdain for their military potential were far from unique among his peers. Until April 1746, this proved to be as ill judged as his confidence in his own army's superiority.

The army that had in its brief existence so disgusted, alarmed, and for a short time threatened to ruin the likes of Hawley can be seen as the culmination of many things. Above all it was the embodiment of the last serious attempt to restore the House of Stuart to the throne of the United Kingdom. It was also the valedictory manifestation of a martial culture peculiar to the Highlands of Scotland. The Army's existence can also be interpreted, in part, as a cry of Scottish patriotic frustration

1. *Oath of Abjuration signed by soldiers of the Duke of Perth's Regiment, swearing allegiance to King James VIII (the Old Pretender) and cancelling any former obligations to King George II - the Elector of Hanover.*

Trustees of the National Museums of Scotland

against the corruption, injustice and perceived loss of independence resulting from the 1707 Act of Union. The Jacobite Army and its campaigns can also been seen as the tragic consequence of cynical foreign interference, reckless opportunism, hopeless idealism and violent exploitation. There were certainly elements of all these present in the Jacobite Army of the '45, but there was also something else which has often been overlooked. Despite the propaganda of the time, this was not simply a rebellious mob – it was an army: organised, recruited, paid and attested as a constitutional alternative to that of the 'usurping prince of Hanover'.

When Charles Edward Stuart chose to launch his campaign to regain his father's throne in the Highlands of Scotland he was not simply looking for the moral support of a few sympathetic land-owners. He and his backers knew that the same geographical and cultural remoteness, compounded by political and economic isolation, that had made many Highland magnates active Jacobites in the past had also preserved their potential to summon up large numbers of fighting men. Although by

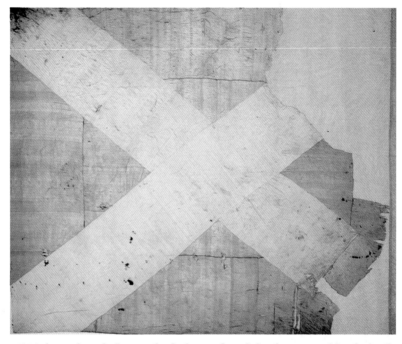

2. Colour of the Stewart of Appin Clan Regiment carried at the Battle of Culloden, April 1746. This is one of very few Jacobite colours to have survived. Those that were captured at Culloden were ceremonially burnt by the public hangman in Edinburgh. The Colour was torn from its staff and smuggled from the battlefield by a soldier of the regiment, Donald Livingstone.

1745 the political climate had changed and far fewer Highland chiefs were willing to risk everything to change their king, enough came forward for Charles and then others, to believe that the game was on. From the very outset then, the core of the Jacobite Army was Highland. This initial support also made it possible for Charles to commission additional regiments from those lowland Jacobites able to raise them. The failure of Charles's assurances of an English Jacobite uprising and a French invasion, which he had made so glibly to encourage the chiefs to join him, meant that from then until the final day at Culloden, the Highland dominance remained.

It says much of Charles and the background to his adventure that he brought with him to Scotland such limited military resources, both in expertise and material. His own military experience was negligible, although he insisted on taking the post of Commander-in-Chief of the army. His principal military advisers were a mixed bag of Irish officers, chosen less for their abilities than for their availability and moral support. Largely ignorant of Scotland and unimpressed by the Highlanders, these men were political exiles who had survived by serving in the armies of any power with whom they had common cause. Unlike the Jacobite Scots, they had little to lose and perhaps much to gain by following Charles. Their lack of understanding for the Scots and the risks they were taking by serving Charles soon led to tension and ill-feeling amongst the senior ranks of the army. Had the conduct of the army been left entirely to them, it is doubtful if much could have been achieved, especially given the army's reliance on its Highland contingent. That this situation was avoided was due in a large part to the role of Lord George Murray as Lieutenant-General of the Jacobite Army. Leaving aside his abilities as a soldier, it was his knowledge and understanding of the Highlanders, and their trust in his leadership, which became a key factor both in keeping the army in the field and in achieving its successes.

When the Highland chiefs rallied to Charles' standard, they simultaneously activated an old and established procedure for transforming the complex network of kinship, patronage and servitude, known as the clan, into a cohesive military unit. With the chief, or his nominee, at its head, his relations and favoured tenants as officers or privileged volunteers, the clan regiment precisely mirrored the social structure of a particular area. As for the ordinary rank and file, it is clear that those at the bottom of the social order had as little alternative to joining their chief's regiment as they had choice in the rest of their lives. Apart from the coercion often necessary to fill the ranks, the other obvious flaw in this smooth and seamless transition was the incorrect presumption that social position and local significance were some guarantee of military experience or particular aptitude.

In the eyes of Charles' advisers, used to the ways of regular armies, this situation soon bred a casual and unmilitary attitude among many of the Jacobite officers. The surviving Order Books of Jacobite regiments are full of impatient and exasperated instructions for regimental commanders to control their men better and organise their officers.[2] As is confirmed by the adoption of conventional military titles, ranks and symbols, Charles was clear in his desire to command a disciplined military body. With the clan regiments at least, such an objective proved almost unattainable.

3. Commission granted to James Colquhoun Grant as a captain in the Jacobite regiment of foot commanded by Colonel John Roy Stewart, signed at Holyroodhouse 27 September 1745. Grant was described as a 'printer and newswriter' in Edinburgh who printed several 'treasonable papers' for the Jacobite cause. Roy Stewart's (Edinburgh) Regiment was recruited from volunteers in Edinburgh and so had a high proportion of committed Jacobites.

In addition to the clan regiments, the Jacobite Army recruited several units in other parts of Scotland. These were raised, commanded and officered by committed Jacobites. Unable to rely entirely on volunteers or on the bonds of clanship to fill their ranks, these regiments made use of any means available to provide recruits. Bribery, threats and sheer force were used, as were the existing legal statutes which forced landowners and communities to provide either recruits or the financial means to enlist substitutes. Desertion from the ranks of the government forces also provided a few recruits. It is therefore clear that ideological commitment was not a major factor in filling the ranks of these regiments. Consequently, desertion was rife (as it was in the clan regiments) and the military capacity of this part of the army was very uneven.

In terms of motivation the mounted units of the Jacobite Army provide some contrast. Numerically small and useful only for scouting duties, they had rather grand sounding titles like Lord Elcho's Life Guards and Baggot's Hussars, again betraying a desperate desire for military respectability. These units were composed of volunteers from a variety of backgrounds, although the requirement either to supply your own horse, or at least have the ability to ride, guaranteed recruits from a higher social class than for the infantry. Consequently, these were men with something to lose by their enlistment, indicating at least some commitment to the Jacobite cause.

The other significant component arrived only after the army was well established. This was the rather speculative contribution of the French government and comprised a number of detachments, or 'picquets', from the various Irish infantry regiments of the French army, together with a single Scottish regiment, the Royal Ecossais. A regiment of cavalry, Fitzjames's Horse, was also sent. Unfortunately, not all these troops actually arrived as planned; a significant proportion were captured on route to Scotland by the Royal Navy. Only about a squadron of Fitzjames's Horse reached Scotland and even they had had to be mounted at the expense of Scottish units; the French, being regular troops, were given a higher priority for the use of the army's limited resources. Despite being regular troops, the French contingents' lack of eventual numbers ensured their presence had little influence over the final fate of the Jacobite Army. Ironically, it was their professional discipline that allowed them their principal contribution to the Rebellion when they covered the Jacobite rear during the final stages of the Battle of Culloden.

If it was hoped that a substantial number of French regular troops could bolster the Jacobite infantry and cavalry, a similar contribution would certainly have transformed their artillery and engineers. Not surprisingly, these were the weakest parts of the Jacobite Army. The artillery train was small, ill-equipped and was little more than an encumbrance to an army forced to cover massive distances during its campaigns. However, Charles attached great importance to its presence, seeing it as a tangible symbol of the army's commitment to his notion of serious warfare. Despite the resourceful use of men with rather tenuously related civilian skills, such as gardeners and carpenters, the Jacobite capacity for field engineering was also weak. Their attempts at a gun battery during the siege of Carlisle were dismissed as 'a poor paltry ditch' by the commander of the Government garrison.[3] Interestingly, considering the success of this siege, one would not normally have expected a defeated commander to play down his opponents' abilities to such an extent. Jacobite attempts before Stirling Castle, under the incompetent direction of a French officer of Scottish extraction, were an utter failure. This was not helped by the refusal of some of the clan regiments to besmirch their Highland dignity by helping to dig trenches.

Apart from confirming the prejudices of the Irish officers, such outbursts of pique must have been a sore trial for those entrusted with the command of the Jacobite Army. Below Charles as Commander-in-Chief, Lord George Murray and the Duke of Perth held equal rank as Lieutenant-Generals. Although Perth had seniority, Murray took much of the actual responsibility. The principal staff appointments went to Captain John William O'Sullivan, an Irish officer of the French service, whose abilities as a soldier and influence with Charles were to be a constant and damaging source of friction with many of the Scots, in particular Lord George Murray. Indeed as the Rebellion progressed, the disharmony between Charles and his most trusted aides and the other Jacobite leaders had a detrimental effect on the morale and performance of the army. This culminated in Charles's decision to take personal command at Culloden and the debacle which followed. For a man like Charles, whose actions were based on an utter belief in his own royal authority and who was closely advised by officers familiar with the ways of European armies, the freely expressed opinions and unpalatable advice offered by his Scottish subordinates became infuriating. According to Murray, he once exclaimed that "It is the obedience of my subjects I desire – not their advice".[4]

During the course of the Rebellion and in its immediate aftermath, government supporters continually attempted to portray the Jacobite Army as a horde of uncivilized barbarians. Given the extent of popular ignorance of, and prejudice against, the Highlanders of Scotland, and

their prominent role in the Jacobite Army, such propaganda was simple work. Yet the Jacobites' attempt to build a military force on a conventional model meant the reality of the Army was rather different from this distorted image. Then, as now, an army exists through discipline; ie the expectation that throughout a chain of command, subordinates will, more often than not, do what they are told. This state is generally achieved through a process of training. Given that the Jacobite Army existed for barely nine months, and was practically in the field for most of that time, the opportunities for organised training were very limited. Yet as the Order Books show, some efforts were made and a certain level of discipline did emerge. In the clan regiments, this was helped by the hierarchical nature of Highland society which predetermined a level of obedience which, although far from perfect, at least existed. Lord George Murray is also credited with devising a simple method of drill which could be easily taught and understood. Certainly, the presence among the regimental officers of men with military experience also had an influence. Although a variety of arms and equipment were in use the bulk of the army was armed with muskets. This alone indicates that a reasonable level of instruction would have been necessary, if only to allow the ranks to load and fire. However, it is clear that even by the later stages of the Rebellion, many Jacobite officers were only too aware of the inadequate training their men had received. This resulted in an over-reliance on the clan regiments and their simple shock tactic of the Highland charge, which although often effective, was recognized as having severe limitations. Despite being issued with targes, indicating a commitment to close quarter fighting, the non-Highland regiments lacked the traditional organisation, arms

5. This contemporary depiction of what appears to be a Highland soldier of the Jacobite Army is not all that it seems. The original plate was produced in London as a portrait of Private Farquhar Shaw of the 43rd Highland Regiment (later the Black Watch), who was one of several soldiers of the regiment executed for mutiny in 1743. By substituting Prince Charles' cypher on the cartridge pouch for that of King George, adding a white cockade and giving him a tartan jacket, an enterprising printer transformed a soldier of the government into a Jacobite rebel. Ironically, the commitment of many of the rank and file of the Jacobite Army to one side or the other was equally transient.

Trustees of the National Museums of Scotland

and skill required to execute the charge effectively.[5] The high turnover of men caused by desertion was also a contributing factor.

This same lack of consistency affected the arrangements for the pay and supply of the Army. In the first weeks of the Rebellion, as the army moved through Scotland and its numbers grew, orders were sent out for the supply of shoes, targes, tents and other items of equipment. At Perth, Lord George Murray ordered that each man was to be supplied with a 'pock' or haversack, so that a daily ration of meal could be issued and carried.[6] This, together with the Jacobite policy of collecting local taxes as the legitimate authority, ensured that the army was at least able to procure a basic level of supplies. It was only when this money ran out and the naval blockade prevented the arrival of any more from France, that the army began to starve prior to Culloden. The same difficulty also meant that by April 1746 the men's pay was hopelessly in arrears. That the Jacobite Army was to be paid at all may still come as a surprise to contemporary readers.

As for the outward appearance of the army, which again was regarded as a definite prerequisite of military credibility, the decision was taken that from the beginning tartan should be worn by the whole army, regardless of territorial origins. There were exceptions to this; the French regulars wore their own uniform and Lord Elcho's Life Guards managed to kit themselves out in handsome blue coats with red facings. Although the Highland garb then had little of the emotional baggage which encumbers it today, its choice by the Jacobite Army was a deliberate attempt to underscore the differences between those who followed the cause and those who opposed it. That the principal of these differences was nationality did much to fix tartan as a new and pervasive symbol of Scotland. Once it had been adopted, Lord George Murray insisted that

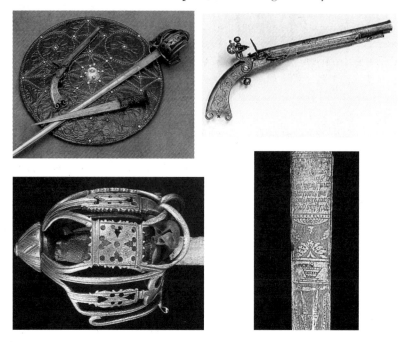

6. Group of weapons typical of those carried by a Highland officer or soldier of the first rank of a clan regiment. These were developed for the close quarter fighting which was the climax of the Highland charge. The targe was carried on the left arm with the dirk or pistol in the left hand and the sword in the right. The sword blade is decorated with a representation of King James VIII and a verse which reads 'With this good sword thy cause I will maintain and for thy sake, O James, will breach each vein'. Both the sword and pistol were taken at Culloden.

the Jacobite officers followed suit as 'as nothing encouraged men more than seeing their officers dressed like themselves and ready to share their fate'.[7]

How then did all these factors affect the performance of the Jacobite Army in action? Despite the variety of military experience among the officers, few had actually seen action. Prior to Prestonpans in September 1745, the same was almost universally true of the rank and file. This inexperience was clearly revealed during this, the first major action of the Rebellion, when the advancing Jacobite line received the one and only salvo from the Government artillery. In the words of one witness, the Jacobite line was seen to give 'a great shake', before steadying itself and continuing the charge.[8]

This basic tactic involved the Jacobites advancing quickly until within a few yards of the enemy, then discharging their muskets. These would then be discarded and the front rank of Highlanders would draw their swords and charge headlong at the stunned enemy line, leaving the other ranks to follow. Once at such close quarters, the front rank Highlander's armoury of sword, pistol, dirk and targe gave him a distinct advantage over conventionally equipped infantry. When pitched against raw troops over favourable ground, the charge was usually very successful, as at Prestonpans and Falkirk. However, if the enemy were better disciplined, the ground flat and soft and the Highlanders' morale and numbers insufficient, as at Culloden, then the outcome was very different. Despite the efforts of its commanders, the Jacobite Army never really had the means or the opportunity to establish any real tactical alternative to the charge. The conduct of the MacDonald regiments at Falkirk perhaps shows best the potential and reality of the Jacobite Army. Faced by the advance of three regiments of Government dragoons, the Jacobite line remained steady and awaited the order to open fire, which was only given when the cavalry were within pistol shot. The effect of this controlled volley stopped the charge dead. Yet in spite of being ordered to hold their position, the Highlanders broke ranks and charged after the retreating dragoons. As a result, three of the army's best regiments took no further part in the action.

Despite all these apparent limitations, the Jacobite Army of the '45 achieved considerable success. Much of this was undoubtedly due to the poor quality of the opposition, especially at the beginning of the Rebellion. The inadequacy of the Government forces deployed in Scotland, and the indifference of many of its supporters, allowed the Jacobite Army to establish itself with the minimum of interference. The desire to take positive action to change their lot, which motivated those who volunteered, gave the Jacobite Army a sense of moral purpose superior to that of the Government forces. However, this early time of opportunity soon passed. The lack of serious military intervention from France and the absence of Jacobite activity elsewhere in the country, quickly left the army isolated and exposed. The shock of its early success had forced a massive redeployment of the Government forces, with troops being rushed back from the Continent, new units organised and

7. Order Book of the Stewart of Appin Clan Regiment, October 1745 to January 1746, giving Charles's orders for 6 December 1745. It would be difficult to find a better example of the bland reassurances and hopeless optimism which so characterised his direction of the Rebellion and his dealings with the commanders of the Jacobite Army, which when these orders were issued had just completed its fruitless expedition to Derby.

Trustees of the National Museums of Scotland

commands reapportioned. By the time all these forces were in place, the Jacobite Army's days were numbered.

The Jacobite Army of the '45 was brought about by the actions of one man, Charles Edward Stuart. Yet it was not his creation. By arriving where and when he did, Charles was able to exploit the circumstances and characters he found with such ease that his improvised army fell almost fully formed into his lap. When circumstances again allowed the army its early success, Charles was once more the unwitting beneficiary. Once the emptiness of his promises of support became apparent, the truly flawed nature of Charles's adventure was revealed. By then it was too late for the army and for the people who created it.

Notes

1. Quoted in full in K Tomasson and F Buist, *Battles of the '45*, Batsford, London, 1962, p 105.
2. Order Book of the Stewart of Appin Clan Regiment, 11 October 1745 to 18 January 1746, Scottish United Services Museum, M.1932.475 and Orderly Book of Lord Ogilvy's Regiment, 10 October 1745 to 21 April 1746, Special Number to Vol II of the *Journal of the Society for Army Historical Research*, 1923.
3. K Tomasson and F Buist, *Battles of the '45*, p 87.
4. K Tomasson, *The Jacobite General*, Blackwood, Edinburgh, 1958, p 31.
5. Orderly Book of Lord Ogilvy's Regiment, p 2.
6. Sir Robert Cadell, *Sir John Cope and the Jacobite Rebellion of 1745*, Blackwood, Edinburgh, 1898, p 89.
7. K Tomasson, *The Jacobite General*, p 35.
8. Sir Robert Cadell, *Sir John Cope and the Jacobite Rebellion of 1745*, p 232.

Chapter Four

KING GEORGE'S ARMY, 1714-1750

Alan J. Guy

'A frugal dispensation'[1]

It is a commonplace that the people of early Georgian England were hostile to standing armies. The legacy of a destructive Civil War, Cromwellian and Stuart 'militarism' and the appearance of war-profiteering in the age of Marlborough obscured an occasional willingness to accept protection offered by local garrisons or take advantage of economic opportunities generated by the presence of soldiers.[2] Moreover, at first, the Hanoverian dynasty, although no armed tyranny, relied upon troops to maintain itself. Margins of victory in the '15 were dangerously narrow and the revelations of the Jacobite 'Atterbury Plot' (1723) provided the occasion for a massive show of government strength in London.

The Prime Minister, Sir Robert Walpole, was probably as keen to manipulate public unease at this time as to pacify it, for he could be disarmingly candid in acknowledging the Whig administration's need for regular troops. A shrewd observer of the unstable European diplomatic scene and always on the look-out for Jacobite intrigue, he exploited genuine fears of war and insurrection to preserve what he believed to be the necessary minimum military force; 18,000 men at home, 2,500 more in the Mediterranean fortresses of Gibraltar and Minorca and another 2,500 or so in the 'Plantations' – New York, Annapolis and Placentia (Nova Scotia), Bermuda, the Leeward Islands and Jamaica. (A separate army, 12,000 strong, not fully integrated into the British administrative system but available as a strategic reserve, was garrisoned in Ireland and funded from the revenues of that kingdom.)

1. King George II at the Battle of Dettingen, 27 June 1743

By John Wootton (1682-1764), c.1743

Accompanied by his son William Augustus, Duke of Cumberland and Robert, 4th Earl of Holdernesse (in profile), who may have commissioned the painting.

Dettingen was fought during the War of the Austrian Succession, 1740-8. At the time of the battle, the British were campaigning in Germany as auxiliaries of Maria Theresa of Austria. Finding his retreat cut off, George II successfully led his British, Hanoverian and Austrian forces against the French inflicting heavy losses. This was the last occasion on which a reigning British monarch led his troops in battle. Cumberland, who greatly distinguished himself in the fighting, was dangerously wounded in the leg.

Reproduced courtesy of the Director, National Army Museum, London

Under the provisions of the annual Mutiny Act units on the British Establishment, although under royal command, were paid for by annual Parliamentary grants. Every year, the Army debate gave frustrated Tories, crypto-Jacobites and country party ideologues in the House of Commons a chance to remind fellow MPs of the threat posed to the rights of free-born Englishmen by a mercenary standing army. These arguments, immensely tedious to listen to, could be refuted without much difficulty, but it was vital to retain the support of the administration's friends, whose loyalty depended on the Land Tax being kept at one shilling in the pound rather than a high-spending rate of four. The result was that military expenditure was cut to the lowest farthing and the cost of what remained sweetened by cultivating the symbiotic relationship between the Army and those sections of the governing classes who provided it with its officers.

This cautious approach to defence spending exerted a profoundly regressive influence on 'military effectiveness' as we would understand it today. Regiments remained 'privatised' in key areas of their pay, equip-ment and weaponry in order to conceal their true cost from the public. As a result the way was left clear for corruption. Company commanders and above had invested in their commands, initially by purchasing at least some of their commissions; they sometimes even found it necessary to support their men out of their own pockets so naturally, whenever money was issued to pay for the Army, they looked after their own interests first. The narrow line between legitimate perquisite and institutionalised fraud could be crossed and re-crossed many times.

The cost-cutting dynamic also ensured that 'small government' prevailed at the centre. The War Office was a tiny department, presided over by superannuated cronies of Walpole and staffed by a handful of clerks. The Pay Office was headed by a Paymaster General whose emoluments came partly from manipulating surplus funds in the Army's central accounts. Much of the drudgery of regimental administration was delegated to non-departmental civilian agents, directly employed by the colonels rather than the Crown, whose income was deducted from regimental funds. The central Government machinery which was supposed to look after manpower-audit and financial control was small and virtually powerless.[3]

Fit for Service?

A 1,000-strong regiment of foot, consisting of up to ten companies, 'topped' with field officers (a colonel, lieutenant-colonel and major) and 'tailed' by staff officers (the adjutant, quartermaster, surgeon and chaplain) was the Army's most important building block, higher formations being organized on an ad hoc basis. A complete regimental structure was always to be preferred, whether for recruiting and training men or for leading them in battle, but the fact that regiments were so expensive (a regiment in the Leeward Islands, 445 strong, with a full complement of 33 officers cost £26 per day; 400 men and ten officers in the four independent companies of New York cost a mere £19 11s 4d), gave the independent company of foot a renewed, albeit barely creditable, lease of life.

Until 1755 these companies were often the only parts of the British Army people living on the frontiers of Empire ever saw. In New York, one company was based in the city itself, but the remaining three were scattered in small detachments as far afield as Albany, Oswego, Saratoga and Schenectady. They were too weak either to guard the invasion route from French Canada, protect the frontier settlements or superintend the fur trade. Their officers enjoyed high status in colonial society, with chances to serve in profitable government posts or engage in the fur trade, but they and their men grew old together, since funds to ship recruits out from home were almost non-existent and very few locals could be tempted to exchange the three shillings a day which could be earned by a working man for the wretched eightpence per diem of a redcoat. There was nobody in authority in New York to check up on the companies' paperwork, so year in, year out, the captains drew for their full pay and mustered them complete. In reality, effective manpower declined from a hundred men per company to less than fifty. Bit by bit the companies merged into their host community and were found to be almost useless when war came.[4]

A broadly similar situation existed throughout Britain's ramshackle first Empire, not least in Scotland, where the establishment of Highland independent companies was disbanded in 1717 on the grounds that the captains had defrauded the public and made deals with the potential rebels and desperadoes their presence on the braes was supposed to watch and control. Six new Highland companies were raised in 1725; funding for them could only be created by reducing men from existing regiments. The new captains were carefully selected, yet the suspicion lingered that they routinely defrauded the public and that the companies were unreliable by their very nature; few of the recruits probably thought of themselves as soldiers in the conventional sense of the term. Predictably, when the outbreak of war with Spain in 1739 raised the possibility of foreign service, dormant ideas of regimenting them were revived.[5]

The new unit, the 43rd Regiment of Foot (later the 42nd) cost the government £15,000 per annum, which underlined the fact that regimentation would not always be the option chosen, even in wartime. In the crisis of the Maroon War in Jamaica (1734), the need for economy had dictated that independent companies were sent to the Caribbean rather than complete regiments[6] while, to modern eyes, the most bizarre of all these improvisations must surely be the drafting of veterans from Chelsea Hospital as marines on Commodore Anson's expedition to the Pacific (1740-4). The selection process quickly degenerated into a cull of the crazy and decrepit, although many of the unlikely circumnavigators had enough sense to desert before the squadron set sail.[7]

Whole regiments were not immune from the degrading effects of this stingy and opportunist management system. The 38th Foot, based in the Leeward Islands from 1707 to 1764, was bankrupted twice (in 1745 and 1752) by the negligence of its commanding officers and civilian agents. Its junior officers (or rather those who could not avoid going to the West Indies in the first place) had to get by on the charity of their planter relatives. The rank-and-file, nominally 400 strong, but greatly reduced by disease, hired comrades to perform their guard duties for them while they took jobs in the civilian community.[8] Closer to home, until the Duke of Cumberland organised a system of regular rotations after 1748, regiments sent to Gibraltar or Minorca also endured lengthy and miserable periods of exile. Tours of duty lasting 20 years or more were not uncommon.[9] In Britain itself, the chronic shortage of troops and their constant use in support of the civil power – suppressing riots or hunting down smugglers, duties which were invariably given priority over combat training – meant that they spent lengthy periods on the march from one location to another, or else dispersed in far-flung country quarters, where the men could only be taught basic arms drill.[10]

The Crown takes control

That such an attritional régime had been partly counteracted by the mid-1740s was a result of personal intervention by the first two Georges, both of whom had impeccable military pedigrees. George II in particular liked to think of himself as a soldier-king: self-satisfaction radiates out from John Wootton's painting of him leading his troops into

2. William Augustus, Duke of Cumberland (1721-65), c.1746

Statuette in lead, by Sir Henry Cheere (1703-81)

The statuette was probably made for a friend or admirer in the period following the Duke's victory at Culloden. It is designed to be viewed from one side only (the heads of both horse and rider face the same direction) and would probably have been placed in an alcove.

Cheere may have used the statuette as a model for his full-sized equestrian statue of Cumberland erected in Cavendish Square, London, in 1770. Commissioned by Lieutenant-General William Strode, it was London's first outdoor statue of a soldier. Taken down for repairs in 1868, the statue was not re-erected, but melted down.

Reproduced courtesy of the Director, National Army Museum, London

action at the Battle of Dettingen (27 June 1743), attended by 'the Martial Boy' – his younger son, William Augustus Duke of Cumberland, soon to be appointed Captain General at the age of twenty-three.

The Hanoverian kings restricted the traffic in commissions, inaugurated a series of financial regulations which limited officers' proprietary control over their commands, introduced improvements in inspection and manpower-audit, imposed new standards of quality and uniformity in military clothing and tried to enforce greater regularity in unit tactics. This process continued fitfully until the century's end, especially during Cumberland's 'peacetime' period as Captain General, which lasted from 1748 until his dismissal in 1757. The central command and administrative infrastructure remained tiny by modern standards however, and senior commanders were members of a patronage network which guaranteed that most of their lucrative perquisites remained intact.[11] Nevertheless, a new appreciation of the importance of 'discipline', coupled with the habituation to wartime conditions resulting from British participation in the Austrian Succession and Seven Years' wars (1740–8, 1756–63), was of decisive importance in the gradual transformation of the army from a congeries of semi-independent parts into a battle-winning instrument with a wide operational repertoire.

'Diamond cut diamond'

The familiar image of 18th century warfare is of long lines of colourfully dressed infantry, ranked three deep, trading musketry three times a minute at ranges of a hundred yards or less. If a regiment managed to deliver one or two well-synchronized volleys in battle, then it had gone a long way towards justifying its existence: the opening British volley at the Battle of Fontenoy (11 May 1745) accounted for more than 700 of the enemy. Such intense fighting probably generated levels of combat stress equal to those experienced in modern warfare, mitigated only by the relative infrequency of pitched battles (disease was the more deadly foe) and a daily existence which was already coarse and brutal – although perhaps not as unremittingly grim as some writers have supposed.[12]

The army got its recruits (volunteers for the most part) from the ranks of the unemployed or, rather, the under-employed who were victims of the fluctuating demand for seasonal labour, together with restless men keen to liberate themselves from humdrum daily life or irksome domestic entanglements. There was no simple equation between economic distress and enlistment, for although the pool of the nation's

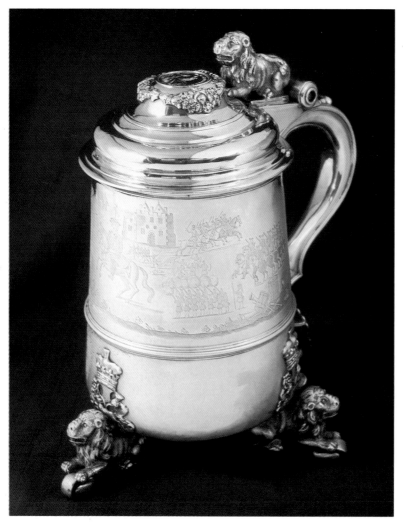

3. Silver tankard commemorating the Battle of Culloden, 16 April 1746

Hallmarked London 1746-7, by Gabriel Sleath (d. 1756)

The tankard, which holds 7 pints of liquid, was made for Cumberland to celebrate his victory at Culloden.

The engraved decoration round the body of the tankard is derived from an engraving entitled 'A Representation of the Battle on Drunmossie Moor near Culloden' [sic], published in London by Henry Overton within a few weeks of the battle. The lid incorporates a silver mortuary medallion, struck by John van Nost in 1765, the year of Cumberland's death, inscribed 'SWEET.WILL.S BLOOM.IS.CLOSD', which suggests an image of Cumberland very different from the 'Butcher' of Jacobite propaganda.

Reproduced courtesy of the Director, National Army Museum, London

unemployed was always bigger than the gaps in the ranks, the regiments struggled to reach their establishment.[13] The pervasive manpower shortage meant that in emergencies it was usually necessary to draft men from one regiment into another going on active service, leaving the parent unit to recruit up to its wartime establishment of 1,000 men. This improvised method of expansion meant that regiments left at home were often depleted numerically, yet with too great a proportion of untrained men in the ranks. This was a potentially fatal combination should they be called into action at short notice, as was the case with Lieutenant-General Sir John Cope's 'green' infantry at the Battle of Prestonpans (21 September 1745), although to be fair to Cope's luckless army, the devastating impact of a well-directed Highland charge could sweep away even seasoned battalions with recent experience of European warfare, as demonstrated four months later at the Battle of Falkirk (12 January 1746).

Armies of the 'old régime' did not have the benefit of staff college training or a readily accessible corpus of doctrine to enable them to respond to such eventualities, but this did not necessarily mean that their commanders were left hopelessly nonplussed or bereft of instructive precedents on which to base their decisions. He may have been caught napping (or more probably lunching) before Falkirk, but Lieutenant-General Henry Hawley had given considerable thought to the best way of neutralising Celtic infantry tactics[14] and the Duke of Cumberland did the same in the invaluable training-time available to him before the Battle of Culloden (16 April 1746), although it is unlikely that many of the soldiers engaged in the terrible hand-to-hand fighting on the left flank of his army had a chance to put their much-trumpeted new bayonet drill into effect.[15]

The practical and psychological importance of artillery in the conduct of 'savage warfare' was also well understood by the 1740s. A decade or so before Culloden, an improvised battery of swivel guns, dragged with immense difficulty over the hostile terrain of the Jamaica back-country, enabled Captain Stoddart to destroy the Maroon stronghold of 'Nannytown': '... having gained a small eminence, commanding the huts in which the negroes were asleep, [Stoddart] fixed his little train of artillery to the best advantage, and fired upon them so briskly, that many were slain in their habitations, and several more threw themselves headlong down precipices. [He] pursued the advantage, killed numbers, took many prisoners, and in short so completely destroyed, or routed the whole body, that they were unable afterwards to effect any enterprize of

**4. Lieutenant-Colonel (later Lieutenant-General) James Adolphus Oughton (1719-80)
37th Regiment of Foot, c.1753**

By George Knapton (1698-1778)

*Oughton is seen here wearing the medal and ribbon of the Cumberland Society, of which he
was Secretary. The Society was founded following the victory at Culloden to celebrate the
Duke's achievements and to mark the end of the Jacobite threat. It met annually on
Cumberland's birthday and Oughton is shown holding a copy of the Society's 'Proceedings'
for 1753.*

*Oughton was commissioned as a juvenile as early as 1734, and served as Major of Brigade at
Culloden. He was commissioned Major-General in 'North Britain' (Scotland) in 1767 and, for
much of the time, acted as Commander-in-Chief there, succeeding to the post itself in 1778.*

Reproduced courtesy of the Director, National Army Museum, London

moment in that quarter of the island' (1734).[16] For his part, Sir John Cope struggled to put together a scratch artillery train before his abortive foray into the Highlands in August 1745 in the belief that it would deter the rebels, and the one ignominious salvo fired by his gunners at Prestonpans did succeed in checking their onslaught, if only for an instant.[17] At Culloden, Cumberland's well-found artillery train, manned for the first time in the campaign by specialists from the Royal Regiment of Artillery, went a long way towards winning his battle for him in the fifteen minutes or so before the two sides came to close quarters.[18]

The important role of fortifications and roads in the suppression of a barbarous opponent seems to have been equally well understood by Georgian soldiers. The post-'15 Highland fortress-building programme at Fort Augustus and Fort George, the creation of fortified infantry barracks at Inversnaid, Kiliwhimin, Ruthven-in-Badenoch and Bernera and the laying-out between 1726 and 1737 of a 250-mile network of military roads forever to be associated with the name of Lieutenant-General George Wade[19] was imitated in the Jamaica of the 1730s by the building of fortified barracks on the fringes of Maroon territory and the establishment of a system of communications between each post.[20]

Like the inhabitants of the Scottish Highlands, the Maroons of Jamaica (the word is probably a corruption of the Spanish *cimarron*, meaning 'wild' or 'unruly', or possibly the French *marron* for 'runaway slave') descendants of slaves of the Spanish, were an 'out-group' of Empire, to whom humane methods of warfare need not necessarily be applied. By the late 1730s British soldiers had been fighting them for a generation. Completely at home in the inaccessible terrain of the interior of the island and able to mingle undetected with the other black and mixed-race inhabitants of the island, the Maroons were masters of the skilfully contrived ambush, rarely wasting a shot, yet almost impervious to the unaimed platoon fire of their regular opponents and endowed with greatly superior mobility. They were said to give no quarter, so it was not to be wondered at that no quarter was offered in return, and if they did not torture their captives, this was only because they were believed to be so quick to butcher them with their cutlasses that there was no time to do so.[21] (Georgian gentlemen had a horror of this type of swordplay, as revealed in their breathless accounts of the wounds inflicted by Highland broadswords at Prestonpans.)

This protracted but little-known war in distant Jamaica also demonstrates that in addition to artillery and forts, the British had other well-tried counter-insurgency tactics available to them long before the experience of the '45. Whereas Scotland had its 'Black Watch',[22] Jamaica had the 'Black Shot' - companies of free negroes assigned to the new forts, and who operated in the interior in conjunction with regular troops and planter militia. In 1737, the government offensive was intensified by importing Indian trackers from the Mosquito Shore, while packs of hunting dogs were already in frequent use. This was a dirty war, with fire and sword liberally applied by the colonial forces, yet it proved impossible to subdue the Maroons except by treaty (1738-9).[23]

In Scotland, in the aftermath of Culloden, the full array of Georgian counter-insurgency techniques was brought to bear to far greater effect than had ever been possible in Jamaica. Methods employed included the bayonetting of rebel wounded, summary executions, the burning of settlements, the confiscation of livestock, and even the threat of mass deportation[24] although, as a milder process of pacification slowly got under way in Scotland, this last idea could be safely rejected. But in other circumstances British commanders would not shrink from this extreme option. Lieutenant-Governor Charles Lawrence stretched his authority beyond the limit by ordering the mass deportation of the 5,000 French inhabitants of Acadia (Nova Scotia) in 1755, yet he was later commended for his zeal and promoted. Lawrence's expulsion of the Acadians was accompanied by the ravaging of their crops, the firing of churches and homesteads and, as an extra ingredient in the cocktail of destruction, breaching the sea-dykes, an action which contaminated the soil of Acadia for years.[25] No amount of genteel whitewashing of Cumberland or the hard men among his followers and imitators should be allowed to cloak the grim realities of the developing Georgian war machine at mid-century.[26]

In Jamaica, the now pacified Maroon war-bands were promptly hired to hunt down escaped slaves – their one-time allies and sympathisers. In Scotland, Highland soldiers were enlisted in large numbers, first for use against their Jacobite fellow-countrymen – a case of 'diamond cut diamond'[27] as Major-General Humphrey Bland put it – and thereafter, once it was realised that raising men for military service offered a way for former Jacobite magnates to rehabilitate themselves, against the King's enemies abroad.[28] Looking back on the Highlanders' martial achievements during the Seven Years' War, William Pitt congratulated himself that having '… sought for merit wherever it was to be found … I found it in the mountains of the north. I called it forth … an hardy and intrepid race of men – men who … had gone well-nigh to have overturned the State in the war before last … They served with fidelity as they fought with valour, and conquered for you in every part of the world'.[29]

There was no denying either their valour in action, or their effectiveness as soldiers. At the bungled assault on the French lines at Fort Ticonderoga, more than 500 of the 1,000 officers and men of the 42nd Foot were killed and wounded (8 July 1758)[30]; fourteen months later on the Plains of Abraham, Fraser's 78th Regiment completed the rout of Montcalm's army by a full-blooded Highland charge, broadsword in hand (13 September 1759)[31], and on the battlefields of the German war (1758-63) Highland soldiers pioneered the kind of light-infantry tactics which would be of such great importance in the development of the art of war towards the end of the century.[32] In retrospect, it is ironic that the extension of the Army's control over the Highlands of Scotland after the '45 resulted in it becoming more genuinely 'British' than ever before.

Notes

1. The phrase is from Richardson Pack's ironical commentary on military economies following the Peace of Utrecht, 'An Epistle from a Half-Pay Officer in the Country to his Friend in London …' written in 1714 and published in 1719; Roger Lonsdale, ed., *The New Oxford Book of Eighteenth Century Verse*, Oxford, 1984, pp 111–12.

2. There is an extensive literature on English anti-army ideology; see in particular Lois G Schwoerer, *No Standing Armies! The Anti-Army Ideology in Seventeenth Century England*, Baltimore and London, 1974. For comment on the role of the army in the localities, see Andrew M Coleby, *Central Government and the Localities: Hampshire, 1649–1689*, Cambridge, 1987, pp68–69.

3. There is a full discussion of these matters in Alan J Guy, *Oeconomy and Discipline: Officership and Administration in the British Army, 1714–63*, Manchester, 1985.

4. For the neglected history of the independent companies of the British Army, see the unpublished study by William A Foote, 'The American Independent Companies of the British Army, 1664–1764', Ph.D. Thesis, University of California, Los Angeles, 1966. For additional material on the New York Companies, see Stanley McCrory Pargellis, 'The Four Independent Companies of New York' in *Essays in Colonial History, presented to Charles McLean Andrews by his students*, Yale, New Haven, 1931, pp 96–123.

5. Andrew Ross, 'The Historic Succession of the Black Watch' in The Marchioness of Tullibardine, *A Military History of Perthshire*, 1908, p48; Bruce Lenman, The *Jacobite Clans of the Great Glen, 1650–1784*, London, 1984, pp99–100; John Prebble, *Mutiny: Highland Regiments in Revolt, 1743–1804*, London, 1975, p29.

6. Foote, op cit, p395–96.

7. Glyndwr Williams, ed., *Documents Relating to Anson's Voyage Round the World* Navy Records Society, London, 1967, pp48–50.

8. For these incidents, see Guy, *Oeconomy and Discipline*, pp88, 151–2.

9. J A Houlding, *Fit for Service: The Training of the British Army, 1715–1795*, Oxford, 1981, pp13–20.

10. Houlding, *op cit*, pp1-98.

11. These developments are discussed in Guy, *Oeconomy and Discipline, passim.*

12. Christopher Duffy, *The Military Experience in the Age of Reason*, London, 1987, *passim.*

13. See the unpublished study by Glenn A Steppler, *The Common Soldier in the Reign of George III, 1760–1793*, Ph.D. thesis, University of Oxford, 1984, *passim.*

14. Katherine Tomasson and Francis Buist, *Battles of the '45*, London, 1962, pp93–94.

15. Rather than bayonetting the Highlander immediately to his front, who might deflect the blow with his targe, the soldier was trained to stab beneath the up-raised sword-arm of the attacker to his right. The hand-to-hand fighting is vividly described by John Prebble, *Culloden*, 1961, pp 100–106, but see the cautious assessments by Tomasson and Buist, *op cit*, p159 and Stuart Reid, *Like Hungry Wolves: Culloden Moor, 16 April 1746*, London, 1994, p38. As a precautionary measure, Cumberland's army had advanced to Drummossie Moor with bayonets fixed; W A Speck, *The Butcher: The Duke of Cumberland and the Suppression of the '45*, Oxford, 1981, p136.

16. Bryan Edwards, *The Proceedings of the Governor and Assembly of Jamaica, in regard to the Maroon Negroes ... containing Observations on the Disposition, Character, Manners and Habits of Life of the Maroons*, London, 1796, ppv–vi. There are a number of conflicting accounts of this action, which was, perhaps, not as destructive as the attackers would have wished; see Carey Robinson, *The Fighting Maroons of Jamaica*, Jamaica, 1969, pp54–55.

17. Tomasson and Buist, *op cit*, pp27, 60–61.

18. There are disagreements as to how long the bombardment lasted, for which see Stuart Reid, *op cit*, pp 92–5, but not as to its destructive effect, vividly depicted by John Prebble, *Culloden*, pp 84–7.

19. For the implementation of this policy, see Lenman, *op cit*, pp96–100; William Taylor, *The Military Roads in Scotland*, Newton Abbot and London, 1976, pp17–23 and Geoffrey Stell, 'Highland Garrisons, 1717–23: Bernera Barracks', *Post Medieval Archaeology*, Vol. VII, 1973, pp20–30.

20. R C Dallas, *The History of the Maroons*, London, 1803, Vol. I, pp38-9.

21. Robinson, *op cit, passim*. The summary killing of prisoners is described by Dallas, *op cit*, p46.

22. The title *Am Freiceadan Dubh* – 'The Black Watch' – was applied colloquially to the Highland Independent Companies; it may have been a reference to the colour of their uniform tartan, or to their duty of suppressing 'blackmail' – payments made in coin or kind in return for 'protection'. Major I H Mackay Scobie believed that the term was first given to the Companies of 1667–1717; 'Early History of the Black Watch', *Journal of the Society for Army Historical Research*, Vol XVIII, 1939, pp126–28. The epithet was apparently not used by the Companies themselves, *ibid*, p128.

23. Dallas, *op cit*, p38.

24. Bruce Lenman, *The Jacobite Risings in Britain, 1689–1746*, London, 1980, pp267–70.

25. For Lawrence's character, see Francis Parkman, *Montcalm and Wolfe*, Library of America edition, New York, 1983, p1021. The severe measures adopted during the expulsion and parallel examples of British 'frightfulness' elsewhere are discussed by Francis Jennings, *Empire of Fortune: Crowns, Colonies and Tribes in the Seven Years' War in America*, New York and London, 1988; see in particular pp178–80.

26. On this controversial topic, compare the generous treatment afforded to Cumberland by his most recent biographer, Rex Whitworth, *William Augustus Duke of Cumberland: A Life,* London, 1992, in particular pp87–96, with the rigorous treatment offered by Speck, *op cit*, pp125–70 and the somewhat less dispassionate account by Lenman, *Jacobite Risings*, pp 260–72. The cultivated brutality of Cumberland and his imitators partly undermined the otherwise beneficial effects of his command as a whole and generated some criticism from within the Army itself; see Alan J Guy, 'The Stubborn English Spirit: Officer Discipline and Resistance to Authority, 1727–1750', *Army Museum '83* National Army Museum, London, 1984, pp31–42. A succession of 'fire and sword' men considered that extreme forms of military government were a universally applicable solution to the problems of Empire. To give but one example, Major John Pitcairn, of Lexington notoriety, considered that in dealing with American colonists, '… one active campaign, and burning two or three of their towns, will set everything to rights'; Pitcairn to the Earl of Sandwich, Boston, 4 March 1775, Henry Steele Commager and Richard B Morris, *The Spirit of Seventy-Six*, Indianapolis and New York, 1958, Vol I, p 62. For a general discussion of this important topic, see Stephen Conway, 'To Subdue America: British Officers and the Conduct of the Revolutionary War', *William and Mary Quarterly*, Vol XLIII, 1986.

27. Speck, *op cit*, p128; see also I H Mackay Scobie, 'The Highland Independent Companies of 1745–47', *Journal of the Society for Army Historical Research*, Vol XX, 1941, pp5-37.

28. Lenman, Jacobite Clans, pp180–212. The first British Army units to fight overseas wearing the Highland dress were probably the two companies of Highland Foot and Highland Rangers, raised in Georgia by Colonel James

Edward Oglethorpe in 1739–40. Both companies probably shared an identical pool of men; Oglethorpe naturally mustered each of them complete; Foote, *op cit*, pp328–44. There are artist's impressions of Highland costume as worn by Oglethorpe's soldiers in Larry E Ivers, *British Drums on the Southern Frontier: The Military Colonization of Georgia, 1733–1749*, Chapel Hill (NC), 1974, pp190–1.

29. Speech of 14 January 1766; Basil Williams, *The Life of William Pitt, Earl of Chatham*, London, 1966, Vol I, p294.

30. Parkman, *op cit*, pp1268–72; Frederick B Richards, 'The Black Watch at Ticonderoga', *Proceedings of the New York Historical Association*, Vol X, 1911.

31. James Michael Hill, *Celtic Warfare, 1595–1763*, Edinburgh, 1983, pp164–66, although note C P Stacey's cautious observation that Fraser's Highlanders may not have caught up with the main body of Montcalm's defeated army; *Quebec 1759: The Siege and the Battle*, Toronto, 1959, p151

32. C T Atkinson, 'Highlanders in Westphalia, 1760-62 and the Development of Light Infantry', *Journal of the Society for Army Historical Research*, Vol XX, 1941, pp208–23

Chapter Five

BATTLES OF THE '45

Stephen Bull

I n the popular imagination the battles of the Jacobite rebellions resound with the sound of the wild Highland charge, followed by the ring of broadsword on bayonet, and when the mêlée is resolved either the red coats flee, or the kilted Scots are slaughtered on the spot. Like so many images it has a grain of truth, but the whole picture is both more complex and less romantic. Sometimes, no doubt, this was how combat was resolved, but it was not how Charles Edward Stuart had intended.[1]

Wherever possible the 'rebel' forces were armed and drilled like regulars. In Bruce Lenman's words the Jacobite force was, 'organised along orthodox lines by professional soldiers'. There were several shipments of French and Spanish flintlock muskets to Scotland, and a certain number of government 'Land Pattern' weapons were also captured, notably from Sir John Cope's army at Prestonpans. Comprehensive data is lacking, but 2,320 muskets were recovered from the field of Culloden and there were issues of ammunition to the troops. On the march into England for example, Lord Ogilvy's regiment received 12 rounds per man.

The same unit had a Franco-Irish regular officer attached, and a Chelsea out-pensioner named James Webster put the men through the drill of the firelock exercise. Webster got away lightly with what could have been construed as treason. Though eventually captured he was discharged by his captors and not executed. By contrast only 190 broadswords were captured at Culloden: doubtless a good number were 'souvenired' by Cumberland's troops, contrary to his instruction, but the point remains that a soldier of the Jacobite army was far more likely to be armed with a musket than a sword. General Hawley seems to have assumed that only the front rank of the opposing troops was equipped with broadswords as well as firearms.[2]

Nevertheless the use of the broadsword captured the public attention. According to a correspondent in the *Gentleman's Magazine*, 'The arms of the Highlanders are a musket, and a broadsword and target; the manner of fighting is to fire at about 30 yards distance, then fling down their muskets, and run in upon the enemy with their swords and targets, and I think their weapons have much advantage of our musket and bayonet, after we have discharged, as they take the point of the bayonet upon their target, and cut at the same time with their broadswords'.[3]

There is good evidence to suppose that the Jacobite leaders thought of conducting their strategies and tactics in a 'modern' manner. The open terrain of Drummossie Muir, for example was 'not proper for Highlanders', as Lord George Murray observed, but ideal for bringing into action artillery, cavalry and the musket. The Prince and some of his advisors, including Quartermaster General John William O'Sullivan, were happy with the ground, and probably chose it in the hope of fighting a successful 'conventional' battle. This important observation does not imply that the Jacobite armies were always used in an unimaginative manner. On the contrary the battles of the '45 show numerous examples of dash and innovation. From the tiny acorn at Glenfinnan grew a force capable of the swift seizure of Edinburgh and the frightening away of two regiments of dragoons, after only the slightest of skirmishes, in the 'Canter of Coltbridge'. The first significant action, fought at Prestonpans on 21 September 1745, is also a case in point in terms of invention. Having failed to get between his enemy and Edinburgh, Sir John Cope took his army of about 2,500 men by ship to Dunbar. Having disembarked he was now determined to defeat the Jacobite force, or effectively to contain them. The Prince's army, similar in strength, marched out to meet him.[4]

Between Prestonpans and the village of Tranent, Cope found a good defensive position with marshy ground to the front. The artillery he placed on his left, and the baggage to the rear. Cope's main strengths were the two dragoon regiments of Hamilton and Gardiner, and his line infantry. These last were not complete regiments, but nine

1. Basket hilted sword, with a hilt by Walter Allan of Stirling. Allan is known to have been active in the 1730s and 1740s, so this type of weapon is likely to have been carried by Jacobites. The blade is marked 'Andria Farara', in a spurious reference to the great Italian swordsmith, but is probably German.

Trustees of the National Museums of Scotland

companies of Murray's, eight of Lascelles's, two of Guise's and five of Lee's. He also had volunteers, some of them Highlanders, who formed a reserve.

Presented with this problem the Jacobite army resolved on a march to outflank the Hanoverians from the east. This they accomplished guided by locals and molested only by some rather desultory artillery fire. Cope was forced to change face, sacrificing his advantageous ground. Given Cope's strength in dragoons a flank march was an eccentric manoeuvre which could have come horribly unstuck, but the result was a remarkable victory. The Hanoverian gunners fled when charged and the cavalry of Hamilton and Gardiner fared little better. According to one account Colonel Gardiner himself was killed with a 'Lochaber axe'. As the rather partisan article in the *Caledonian Mercury* explained, ' The signal having been given to form and attack, nothing could parallel the celerity and dexterousness with which the highlanders perform'd that motion, except the courage and ardour with which they afterwards fought; and pulling off their bonnets, looking up to heaven, made a short prayer, and ran foward. They received a very full fire from right to left of the enemy, which killed several; but advancing up, they discharged and threw down their muskets, and drawing their broad swords gave a most frightful and hideous shout, rushing most furiously upon the enemy; so that in seven or eight minutes both horse and foot were totally routed'.

2. *Fully armed, and traditionally clad, Highland soldier and corporal of the mid-18th century. Jacobite troops would have been lucky indeed to match the musket, bayonet, pistol, broadsword and dirk seen here. In this period most edged weapons were worn suspended from a shoulder belt, although dirks were often worn centrally on the waistbelt.*

From Military Antiquities Respecting a History of the English Army, *Francis Grose, 2nd edition, 1812.*

Glasgow Museums

The Highlanders under Lord George Murray on the left appear to have got into action first, while the Duke of Perth's regiment came up on their right, and although Colonel Whiteford managed to discharge some of the abandoned guns the charges were not to be stopped. Cope and Lords Loudoun, Drummore and Home made some attempt to rally their commands but a general rout set in as the MacDonalds were now lapping around the Hanoverian left. The Jacobites had lost only 50 or so, but the government forces had suffered a disaster. About 300 were killed and 1000 taken into captivity at Prestonpans which at the time was known as the Battle of Gladsmuir.[5] Some commentators blamed the defeat on complacency and overconfidence. Mist, poor intelligence and pure terror added up to a defeat which would result in two and a half centuries of mockery for 'Johnnie' Cope.[6] The way to England was now open; but the recruiting there would be poor, and not more than a few hundred would ever join the colours. Even with limited French and Irish help the Jacobite army would number under 6,000 and Charles Edward would fight no major battle on English soil. William Augustus, Duke of Cumberland and commander of the Hanoverian forces, wanted to bring the enemy to battle on ground of his own choosing, and duly prepared his forces at Stone, north of Stafford. This effectively blocked the route to Wales, but the Prince wisely refused this invitation.

The council held at Derby on 5 December 1745, has been identified as a critical moment of decision. The Prince still believed that the opposition would be toppled by a last push, but his generals were more concerned that they were dangerously close to being trapped and crushed by overwhelming odds. In reality Cumberland was himself worried and frustrated and his troops were not quite as numerous or well placed as the Jacobites believed. Nonetheless to press on now would have been a pure gamble, and the Prince's generals did not even have the information with which to calculate the odds. The skirmish at Clifton near Penrith, fought on 18 December 1745 during the Prince's retreat back to Scotland, showed élan in the face of adversity. Lord George Murray's rearguard of Highlanders made good use of hedges whilst skirmishing with the enemy dragoons and the volunteer 'Liverpool Blues'; when darkness fell he attacked, driving off the opposition. It was a minor action but one which helped to buy a little time for the Prince's main body.

General Hawley, who had replaced Wade as commander of the force pursuing the Jacobites, had a good idea of the problems which beset his army, and on 12 January 1746 issued the following description of the enemy tactics – 'They commonly form their Front rank of what they call their best men, or True Highlanders, the number of which being allways but few, when they form in Battallions they commonly form four deep, & these Highlanders form the front of the four, the rest being lowlanders and arrant scum. When these Battallions come within a large

Musket shot, or three score yards, this front Rank gives their fire, & Immediately thro' down their firelocks & come down in a cluster with their Swords & Targets making a Noise & Endeavouring to pearce the body, or Battalions before them becoming 12 or 14 deep by the time they come up to the people they attack.' In his opinion the way to deal with such an assault was with a steady three rank line. The rear rank of the line should commence firing at the centre of the enemy body at only 12 paces, followed by the rest at point blank range. Firing sooner was suicide because the Highlanders would close rapidly not giving time to 'load a second Cartridge'. The troops should do their best to put from their minds the 'lyes' spread about enemy invincibility.

Back in Scotland the Prince's army was much reinforced and attempted, ineffectually, to reduce Stirling. Hawley marched up to confront them and the 'rebels' established themselves on Plean Muir. The Jacobites now resolved to march on Hawley's forces by two different routes and thus gain advantage of higher ground from which to attack. The daring plan for a while appeared to teeter on the edge of disaster, when discovered by officers of Howard's regiment, alarmed by a countryman. Hawley rapidly moved his force, 8,000 strong, and numerically a match for the Jacobites, on to Falkirk Muir.[7]

With his dragoons thrown foward on the left Hawley's infantry was deployed in two lines of six regiments each, Wolfe's, Cholmondley's, Pulteney's, the Royals, Price's and Ligonier's to the fore, and Blakeney's, Munroe's, Fleming's, Barrel's, Battereau's and Howard's behind. Scottish volunteers and Militia were placed on the left and right. The advancing Jacobites were similarly in two major lines the front line being formed by the Appin Stewarts, Camerons, Frasers, MacPhersons, Mackintoshes, Mackenzies, Farquharsons and MacDonalds in the 'place of honour' on the right of the line. The second line was made up of Gordons, Ogilvy's and the Atholl brigade.

'Hangman' Hawley now unleashed Colonel Ligonier's command of dragoons. With commendable steadiness the Jacobites stood and gave a close range volley. This caused enough gaps that watchers behind could 'see daylight' through the ranks, and now the Prince's men surged foward, and the dragoons wheeled back. Rain was begining to dampen Hanoverian powder and as the MacDonalds charged home the Glasgow volunteers routed. Now Hawley's left was hard pressed and began to crumple, and men began to stream to the rear. Cholmondeley's regiment, which had appeared calm at the outset, now collapsed completely.

On the right Ligonier's, Price's and Barrel's were giving a better account of themselves. Their fire continued, and a rough cohesion was kept as they first advanced and then retired. They even managed to secure a prisoner in the shape of Major MacDonald of Tiendrish, who in the smoke and confusion had run up to join them, believing them to be his own men. In about half an hour it was all over, the Hanoverians had lost over 600 killed, wounded and captured whilst the Jacobites, who had less than 200 casualties, went on to occupy Falkirk. In the dark many of the dead were stripped of their uniforms and valuables; one spectator recalled seeing them like 'a large flock of white sheep' stretched out on the hillside.[8]

Falkirk had been a victory but the Prince was still in retreat. At the end of January Cumberland arrived in Edinburgh, and as the noose tightened the Prince was forced back on the Highlands. In the bad weather the Hanoverian army now manoevered to concentrate at Aberdeen. A surviving Order Book of Cumberland's army at Aberdeen provides a picture of a well organised force under draconian discipline.[9] The infantry were divided into five brigades, each of three regiments under brigade majors. On 15 March a parade was held, the regiments receiving the duke 'three deep in open order with the Grenadier company on the right', and after Cumberland had passed through the ranks were solemnly closed. Sentries and pickets were posted in strength and passwords in the form of the names of British towns were issued daily. Such was the state of readiness demanded that on occasion the whole army slept in tents and billets without removing their clothes or accoutrements.

Returns were made of men lost in action, prisoners and wounded. Arms were also counted and deficiencies rectified, and each man was issued with 24 rounds of ammunition. Bread ovens were built of brick, by bricklayers drawn from the ranks, and regular rations baked. Plunder, 'marauding', taking firewood without orders, selling bread and gaming were all strictly prohibited. Courts martial were a common occurrence and amongst those unfortunate enough to be caught committing offences were three soldiers sentenced to 1000 lashes and a fourth to 500. Francis Massey of Wolfe's regiment was hung for desertion. Neither were officers spared tough discipline, and though their punishments were more gentlemanly, more than one was cashiered. Fines were also taken, and the money used for 'the hospital'. Quartermaster Wright of Howard's regiment had not only to pay back what he embezzled but lose six months pay.

Training was not ignored; each regiment was taken 'out at exercise' in turn, and put 'through the manual'. Recruits and 'awkward men' had a particularly hard time being taken out twice a day. In the case of some particularly poor specimens sent up from Newcastle, these were dismissed immediately with three weeks pay in their hands. Firelock drill received attention and in the case of Grant's Highlanders 'a proper man and if possible a highlander', was nominated from Barrel's regiment for their training.[10]

In early April campaigning began again in earnest, Cumberland crossed the Spey and marched in the direction of Inverness. At Nairn, after a brief skirmish, he encamped, and the rest of the Jacobite army emerged from Inverness to confront him. The ground selected for the coming battle was Drummossie Moor; at the time this was an open stretch of moorland, bounded on one side by bogs and Culloden Parks, and on the other by walled enclosures and the water of Nairn. For an army contemplating a regular and 'modern' defensive action it would have been a reasonable choice. Artillery could have been placed to sweep the open ground, dismounted dragoons would have lined the enclosures, and a strong cavalry reserve kept against emergencies. Unfortunately the Jacobite force was not such an army; their artillery was weak, their horse relatively few in number, and their infantry temperamentally disposed to the attack. Lord George Murray implored the Prince to consider more rugged ground across the river Nairn, but to no avail.

On 15 April, with no sign of Cumberland advancing to the selected spot and the rebels short of food and supplies, the sort of plan which had won Prestonpans and Falkirk was hatched. That evening they would march under cover of darkness to the Hanoverian camp and take their slumbering enemies, who were thought to have been celebrating the Duke's birthday, by surprise. The strategy was not without serious risks, but it was viable. With the night march the Prince's luck simply ran out; it took too long. Faced with the probability of appearing after dawn as a distended straggling column in front of Cumberland's rested and ready men the plan was called off. Back on Drummossie the Jacobite army was now in a worse position than before, tiredness and hunger were now

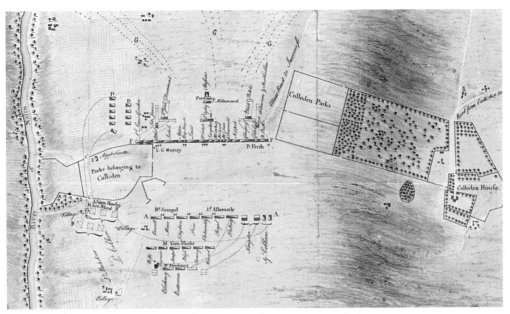

3. Plan of the Battle of Culloden 16 April 1746. This accurate map was painted by Paul Sandby and is dated April 23 1746.

The Royal Collection © Her Majesty The Queen

verging on exhaustion and starvation, and there were more stragglers than ever. The number of Jacobites who fought at Culloden is unlikely to have been much more than 5,000, the cavalry component of which was about 350. There are thought to have been 14 rather ill-assorted field pieces with the army, although the Finlayson plan shows only nine.[11]

The infantry was laid out in two major lines about nine hundred yards long, blocking the gap between the walled enclosures on either side of the field. The front line, which was by far the stronger of the two, was composed, right to left, of the Atholl brigade, the Camerons, the Stewarts of Appin, the Frasers, Mackintoshes, Farquharsons (Monaltrie's battalion), the combined regiment of the MacLachlans and MacLeans, the Chisholms, and finally, on the left and in a position not particularly to their liking, the various MacDonald clans. In the second rank, again right to left, were the battalions of Stonywood, Lord Ogilvy, John Roy Stuart, Kilmarnock's guards, the Ecossais Royal, the Irish, Glenbucket's regiment and the Duke of Perth's. The terms 'regiment' and 'battalion' can only be taken in the loosest context, for 5,000 infantry were divided into over 20 small units, the strongest of which can scarcely have exceeded 300. The tiny cavalry squadrons were held back, and the guns were deployed in three batteries, one on each side and one to the centre front of the army. Plans of the Jacobite dispositions, both contemporary and modern, vary in detail; this is probably because of the smallness of some of the bodies and also because their relative positions would change.

Cumberland's army had struck camp by five and headed off in three columns. About nine they received intelligence of the enemy position which came into view a couple of hours later. The Hanoverian army has been estimated at about 8,000 strong, the bulk of which were the infantry regiments. These were deployed initially in three lines, which were later readjusted to two.[12] As they were finally stationed the front rank was composed of Pulteney's, the Royals, Cholmondeley's, Price's, the Scots Fusiliers, Munroe's and Barrel's. Next to Barrel's on the extreme left Wolfe's regiment was positioned so as to flank the line and provide enfilade fire in the event of attack. The field guns were in five pairs along the front rank. In second line, right to left were Battereau's, Howard's, Fleming's, Bligh's, Sempill's and Ligonier's. Blakeney's formed a final reserve to the rear, and the dragoons, light horse and militia secured the flanks ready to thread their way around and through the walled enclosures.

The battle began just after one with an exchange of cannon fire which caused a momentary halt to Cumberland's dragoons; but the damage rendered by the Jacobite batteries was slight compared to the shock. Colonel Belford's Hanoverian artillerists, who were better trained and supplied, now started to tear holes in the Jacobite ranks. The unpleasantness was added to by a rain squall, and ball bounced and scudded right through to the rear of the Prince's position. Here several of Baggot's Hussars were cut down. It was soon apparent that the Jacobite army was going to have to choose between attack and retreat, for simply to stand under bombardment in open terrain was tantamount to a slow suicide. After a little heart-searching the order to attack was sent, but the bearer was decapitated by a roundshot. Most of the clansmen carried on waiting and dying until Brigadier Stapleton arrived with a repeat order, although the Atholl brigade who were closest to their enemy may have literally jumped the gun and begun to move early.

The Jacobite line now boiled foward but the charge was botched. There was no element of surprise and the attackers, not being parallel to their target, were at different distances from the Hanoverian front. The MacDonalds on the left, furthest from their antagonists in Pulteney's and the Royal Scots never reached their opponents. In the centre the

4. The King's Colour of Barrel's Regiment, carried at Culloden. Depicted on the centre of a union flag is a crowned lion statant gardant, standing on a royal crown, over crossed sceptres. Since neither this, nor the matching 'colonel's' or 'regimental' colour, which also survives, conform to the royal warrant of 1743, it is likely to have been made prior to that date. Originally raised in 1680 in the London area and the west of England for the defence of Tangier, this regiment would later become the 4th of Foot.

Mackintoshes and Frasers drifted to their right, perhaps because this was the shortest route to the nearest enemy, or because the going was better underfoot and they were already staggering under the fire of Cholmondeley and Price's regiments.

As the Highlanders came on the Hanoverian gunners switched from ball to case shot. Far from faltering in the face of the charge much of Cumberland's front line held its fire and delivered a shattering volley; Munroe's and Barrel's being delivered at particularly close range into the Atholl men, whilst Wolfe's regiment raked their flanks. Amazingly, after such treatment, the attackers carried on, their momentum taking them into and around Barrel's and Munroe's foot. Captain Lord Robert Kerr of Barrel's took a charging Highlander on his 'spontoon' or polearm, only to have his own head 'cleft from crown to collar bone'. Some of the Jacobites now managed to pierce the enemy front line. Lieutenant Colonel Rich, commanding Barrel's was himself cut down, one hand severed, and the other arm nearly cut through at the elbow. He also suffered six head wounds. Barrel's grenadier company was forced backwards, and Ensign Brown was wounded and floored but refused to

let go of the colour. At this vital moment with the Highlanders 'fighting like furies' and Barrel's 'behaving like heros', the second line opened up.[13]

Major General Huske had brought foward Bligh's and Sempill's regiments in support and now they poured in fire. More than likely a few of their comrades in the front line were also shot, but it was a decisive move. Michael Hughes, a volunteer with Bligh's, saw Highlanders stabbed with the swords of officers, and the polearms of sergeants, as well as rammed through and skewered by bayonets. The Stewarts of Appin, Camerons and Atholl men were all hard hit. Dougal Stewart, the ensign carrying the 'Appin Banner', was killed; three more in their turn raised the colour and were shot down. The precious flag was saved only when Donald Livingstone, otherwise known as 'hairy Donald', rescued it in the retreat.[14]

Whilst carnage continued, the militia and dragoons were filtering their way through the dry stone walls on the Jacobite right flank, breaking holes in the enclosures and harassing Lord Lewis Gordon's men who were attempting to fend them off. On the other flank Kingston's horse were threatening the MacDonalds, effectively pinning them, since if the clansmen charged now there was a danger that they would be crushed between the horse and Pulteney's foot. The Prince's army , blasted and bludgeoned to a standstill, now began to waver. The Hanoverians began

5. *Laurie and Whittle's print of the battle of Culloden, published in London 1797. The original caption reads 'This view of the glorious victory obtained over the rebels shews his Majesties army commanded by His Royal Highness the Duke of Cumberland, drawn up in three lines; the front consisting of six battalions of foot, the second of five, the third was a body of reserve, composed of four. Part of the Highland army is here represented as furiously attempting with swords and targets to break in upon the left of the Duke's front line, where their rashness*

68

to advance and the horse were unleashed upon the confused and disrupted units of the enemy. In most battles more casualties are suffered by the defeated in their rout than in the battle proper, and in this Culloden was to be the rule rather than the exception. Where Culloden differed, and was to become infamous, was in the attitude of the victorious general. Within hours Cumberland ordered his men to search out surviving rebels, in the 'neighbourhood of the field of battle', reminding his troops, dubiously, that the rebels had orders to 'give us no quarter'.

In the light of such incitement and the furious discipline of the army it was more remarkable that a few brave souls should have refused the invitation to kill, rather than that a good number accepted. There were also those who turned a blind eye or preferred plunder to violence, like the two sentries who, for the contents of his purse, allowed a wounded man his life. Another distinction of Culloden was that most of the Jacobite army were perceived by the victors as rebels, rather than enemy soldiers. That atrocities were committed cannot be denied. Civilians were cut down during the pursuit by English dragoons but one should not assume that the motivations were simply anti-Scottish. Some of the worst incidents were Scot on Scot, or Lowlander on Highlander, or between clans of historic rivalry. A detachment of the Royal Scots was witnessed to shoot wounded prisoners; Campbells set to looting. Mythologising started even before the bodies were cold; certain Jacobites, including Gillies MacBean and John MacGillivray, were credited with large numbers of Hanoverian dead. Total casualties on the government side were however under 400, many of whom were wounded; the Prince's army lost in excess of 1000.

It is significant that Cumberland would become known not only to Jacobites as 'the Butcher', it was also a tag accorded him by his opponents in England. Given the will, he could well have made sure that few if any atrocities took place, but what was initiated at Culloden was later to become a more widespread suppression of Highland culture. Curiously the victory also brought out the best in the Duke's character as well as the worst; every wounded man in his army received 12 guineas from his private purse, and 16 went to every man who captured an enemy colour. Soldiers in custody were all released. Captured colours and guidons were now taken to Edinburgh to be burned. The Jacobites had learned the hard lesson of many a war; that several battles might be won, but one defeat could lead to catastrophe.[15]

Notes

1. Several modern works are most useful for the campaigns and battles of the '45, amongst them K Tomasson and F Buist, *Battles of the '45*, London, 1962, new edition with corrections, London, 1967; J Prebble, *Culloden*, London, 1961; and F J McLlynn, *The Jacobite Army in England*, Edinburgh, 1983. All have bibliographies. Generally useful is R C Jarvis *Collected Papers on the Jacobite Risings*, Manchester, 1972. Interesting sidelight on the campaigns is provided by N Woolf *The Medallic Record of the Jacobite Movement*, London, 1988. For Jacobite prisoners and casualties see A Livingstone, C W H Aikman and B S Hart (eds) *Muster Roll of Prince Charles Edward Stuart's Army 1745–1746*, Aberdeen University, 1984. The Public Records Office information sheet *Sources for the History of the Jacobite Risings*, No 4, 1986, is a good starting point for a more detailed study.

2. Such is the point of view argued by S Reid in 'The Jacobite Army at Culloden', in *Military Illustrated*, numbers 36 and 38, 1991, and in *Like Hungry Wolves, Culloden Moor, 16 April 1746*, London, 1994. A number of the original documents from which the evidence is drawn are reprinted in the Spalding Club series. On the subject of French involvement see F J McLynn *France and the Jacobite Rising of 1745*, Edinburgh, 1981. For swords see A Campbell *Scottish Swords From the Battlefield At Culloden*, new edition E A Mowbray ed. Providence, 1971.

3. *The Gentleman's Magazine*, Vol XV, October 1745, p 527.

4. A detailed analysis of Cope's forces is given in R C Jarvis Vol 1, pp25–47, including Colonel Whitefoord's figures which are now part of British Library *Add. Mss.* 36592. See also R Cadell *Sir John Cope and the Rebellion of 1745*, Edinburgh, 1898. Jacobite army lists for all three major battles of the '45 appear in Livingstone, Aikman and Hart, *op cit*, pp 216-219.

5. *Gentleman's Magazine*, pp 588-589. Tomasson and Buist, *op cit*, pp 60–80. P Doddridge *Some Remarkable Passages in the Life of the Honourable Col. James Gardiner*, London, 1747, *passim*. H Blackburne *Historical Record of the 14th (King's) Hussars*, London, 1901, pp14–16. There are several popular 'battlefield' books which give accounts of this and other actions; the most useful of these being D Smurthwaite *The Ordnance Survey Complete Guide to the Battlefields of Britain*, Exeter, 1984, and W Seymour *Battles in Britain*, Vol.2, London, 1975.

6. *The Report of the Proceedings and Opinion of the Board of General Officers on. . .Sir John Cope*, London, 1749.

7. Some commentators regard Falkirk as a lost opportunity despite the victory, for example F J McLynn *Bonnie Prince Charlie*, Oxford,1991, pp 207-222. See also L I Cowper *The King's Own*, Oxford, 1939, pp 174–8. On militia and volunteers see Jarvis pp97–171.

8. Tomasson and Buist, *op cit*, pp99–132

9. Order Book of Barrel's Regiment, March–April 1746, King's Own Regimental Collection, Lancaster City Museum, 880–3. Special thanks are due to Peter Donnelly, for his assistance in tracing this document.

10. *Ibid*. The specific numbers of breeches and shirts issued under the 'Veteran Scheme' after Culloden are also listed here for six regiments; the Royals 568, Barrel's 458, Price's 416, Scots or 'North British' Fusiliers 473, Cholmondeley's 534, Monroe's 566, and these figures may indicate the numbers surviving. They are noticeably higher than the figures given in Major Bendyshe's notebook cited in C T Atkinson, 'Culloden', *Journal of the Society of Army Historical Research*, Vol XXXV, 1957, p19, but it may be that the former represents the whole regiment whilst the latter includes only those actually present on the field. If this is so Cumberland's army at Culloden was no more than 7,000.

11. The various plans extant include Yorke's, drawn by an aide-de-camp to Cumberland and now in the British Library (*Add Mss* 35,889 f 105), Finlayson's , drawn by John Finlayson, Jacobite artillery officer and instrument maker, and Campbell's; see I C Taylor, *Culloden: A Guidebook to the Battlefield with the Story of the Battle*, Edinburgh, 1965, (fifth revised edition 1972) pp 28-31. There are also contemporary annotated engravings of the battle including the *Representation of the Battle on Drummossie Moor Near Culloden*.

12. Prebble, *Culloden* pp76–134; McLynn, *Bonnie Prince Charlie,* pp249–64; Tomasson and Buist *op cit* pp143–204; Young P and Adair J, *Hastings to Culloden*, Kineton, 1979, pp255–78. From the point of view of the visitor Culloden is probably the most rewarding of the '45 battlefields. Much of the forest which later covered the site has been cleared since 1980, and there is a modern Visitor Centre. Memorials and grave stones may also be seen, though the attribution of individual clans to each plot is open to question since the markers were not erected until 1881. It is also arguable that the total extent of the battlefield was larger than that prescribed by the recent signposting.

13. Cowper, *op cit*, pp182–6. Atkinson, *op cit*, pp18–19.

14. B Smyth, *A History of the Lancashire Fusiliers*, Dublin, 1903, pp78–9. R Cannon, *Historical Record of the Twentieth or East Devonshire Regiment of Foot*, London, 1847, p14.

15. See J Prebble, *The Highland Clearances*, London, 1963, *passim*. Tomasson and Buist, *op cit*, pp205–11.

Chapter Six

JACOBITE CULTURE

Murray G. H. Pittock

THE Jacobite cause is famous in history, arguably for the wrong reasons. Our understanding of its significance is damaged in two ways: by the romanticism surrounding its status as a colourful lost cause, and not less by attempts to 'correct' this view, which portray the Jacobite risings as minor, marginal struggles in a sordid dynastic civil war as opposed to chivalrous if doomed attempts to defend the Scottish identity. Both the myth and the attack on the myth of Bonnie Prince Charlie lack a grasp of the variety and detail of Jacobitism, which a study of Jacobite culture can provide.

One of the chief errors of the above views is to lay undue emphasis on the Highland nature of Jacobitism. There are reasons for this emphasis, aside from any confusion between Scotland north of the Forth and the Highlands, or the distinction between the uniform and background of the Jacobite army. First, Jacobite culture can be both romanticised and marginalized by confining it within the orbit of the vanished world of pre-Clearance clan society. Secondly, the social, political, linguistic, geographical and even the religious relevance of the risings is reduced when Jacobitism is described as 'Highland' or 'Catholic'. Thirdly, a purely Highland Jacobitism gives a spurious clarity to the view of the Jacobites as defending a vanishing way of life, whether or not this is presented in romanticised terms. Sceptical historians have until recently described the Jacobite forces as if they were savages, while on the romantic side they are still presented as Gaels fighting a last battle to defend their ancient civilisation.

In the ensuing brief introduction, it will be seen that the diversity of Jacobite culture and the context of its ideas do not match up to these familiar preconceptions. An examination of the evidence reveals at least three kinds of Jacobite culture. First, there is the high culture of the aristocracy, gentry and intelligentsia (including the Church), which inherits a political and monarchical ideology from before the Revolution of 1688-9, and continues to defend it thereafter. Essentially conservative, this group nevertheless has strong traditional contacts with the poorer members of society which it has to depend on even more when some of its members (eg the Episcopal clergy) are criminalized and reduced to poverty. A formerly powerful class is deprived and dispossessed insofar as its members continue to espouse and act on their beliefs. Although prevalent in Ireland and Scotland, this kind of Jacobite culture is found throughout the British Isles. Its ideas, based on a shared European high culture of classical and biblical typology, do not greatly differ in (for example) English and Gaelic. Ironically, perhaps, the Highland chieftain class were among the least vulnerable members of this group prior to 1745. As at least one leading historian of the period has noted, the clan leaders may be seen to have taken a more self-interested view of the Rising in that year than did their Lowland Episcopalian counterparts. In this context it is worth remembering that not much more than half of Charles's army was made up of clan units.

Secondly, and of at least as much interest, is the strength of Jacobite ideology in folk and popular culture. Whereas high cultural Jacobitism can be found in artefacts almost as readily as in poetry or sermons, its folk and popular counterpart is (for obvious reasons of cost) far more rooted in music, oral and written verse, the coded or explicit cries of the mob and popular symbolism such as the use of flowers, rural pursuits, or the burning of Hanoverian 'guys' in public demonstrations of Jacobite support. The display of Jacobite ideas and values from this end of the social spectrum was more often radical, as might be expected. Indeed, many of the areas which witnessed Jacobite unrest in the earlier 18th century were centres of radical activity in the French Revolutionary period, and it has been suggested that political protest in early 19th century England could have based itself on Jacobite models.

The third area of Jacobite culture worth exploring is what has been called the cross-class interchange between the two groups examined above. High and folk/popular Jacobite culture had interests which converged: most obviously the restoration of the Stuart dynasty, but also (in parts of Scotland and Ireland especially) more favourable terms for Episcopal or Catholic worship and the return of national autonomy. In addition to these shared aims, other circumstances served to reinforce cultural commonalty. In the first place, high cultural Jacobites often held views inimical to the financial revolution, land enclosures and other social developments which increased mobility and threatened rural communities. The idealisation of rural values and folkways in Jacobite writing dated back to the early 17th century at least. Whereas the urban Whig Hanoverian regime could be associated with the destruction of folk culture (as in Henry Fielding's case), the Jacobite gentry nurtured it through the castle culture which replaced that of the court in Scotland after 1603, and by the patronage of bards like Aogan Ó Rathaille in Ireland and Sir Watkin Williams Wynn's Welsh minstrel. A socially conservative outlook (which could be radical in its application to 18th century politics) lessened the growing distance between the culture of the folk and the gentry. It was only when Jacobitism was politically defeated that a later generation found itself ready to return to folk culture in the safely distanced and marginalized guise of primitivism.

Secondly, the criminalization of Jacobitism drew high and folk cultural elements together. Severe penalties awaited the convicted Jacobite, of whatever social class and the last arrest (of Count Rohenstart) was not until 1817, though prosecutions were dying out by the 1770s. Drawn together by a common fate (indeed in 1746 some two-thirds of those executed were from the officer class), Jacobites from differing social groups shared more than divided them. In addition, their criminal alliance extended beyond the treason of which the state proclaimed them guilty. It was argued by a major Jacobite ideologue, Chevalier Ramsay, that if hereditary right is denied in kingship, it loses its security in property: bad title to the crown rendered all inheritance insecure. In denying the necessary legitimacy of Hanoverian property laws, many Jacobites were challenging the validity of the regime's criminal justice system. This could bring them into sympathetic contact with a criminal underclass (as in the strong associations between Jacobitism and smuggling): it could also make them members of that class themselves, as in the case of Thomas Butler, the highwayman and Jacobite spy. It could be argued that such figures were merely taking advantage of the bogus property rights built up since 1688. A report sent to James VIII and III in 1728 identifies destitution (caused by inequitable distribution of property) as a major cause of crime. The unstable basis of property is reflected in much of the literature of the period, not least John Gay's quasi-Jacobite *Beggar's Opera*, where the highwaymen allude to William II and III's conquest in 1688 to legitimise their own use of force. The perceived gentlemanly status of highwaymen (to some extent justified by the facts) underlined the instability of social and economic relationships in the post-1688 era, when thousands of soldiers of James VII and II's army who had refused to serve under William may have been at large in England. On the margins, Jacobitism forced divergent social and political groups together in a cultural exchange: hence in the 1740s and 50s, English Tory gentleman sported the badge of the impoverished Gaeltacht in wearing tartan at fashionable meets and resorts such as Bath. In 1743, Sir John Hynde Cotton even ordered a bespoke set of tartans to proclaim his Stuart patriotism.

Such actions amplified and publicised the views of high society Jacobitism, whose coded critiques of post-1688 society had long been able to stir popular interest, as when the high Anglican priest Sacheverell's crypto-Jacobite sermon *The Perils of False Brethren* sold 100 000 copies (50 000 in the first three weeks) in 1709–10. The Jacobite culture of this disenchanted ruling group centred on three major themes: the sacramental authority of Stuart monarchy in the context of an Anglicanism which had substituted Crown for Papacy in the 1530s; the hereditary right of the Stuarts enshrined in the classically-derived Brut myth; and the identification of the king as a magical monarch capable of restoring his realms and the lives of his subjects from poverty to plenty. This third category drew on that element in Scoto-Irish foundation myth which saw the monarch as male and his land as female: and all three themes drew on the deep-seated connotations of the King's Two Bodies: the idea that the king had both a sacred and secular role and identity.

In terms of the monarchy's sacramental status, the Papacy's struggle with regal authority had a long history, dating back to the Roman Empire, and exemplified in forgeries such as the Donation of Constantine and letters like that of Gregory VII in 1081, denying miraculous power to kings. In seeking to replace pope by king, Anglicanism placed itself on the regal side of this controversy. Certain ceremonies, such as the Royal Touch, the healing of the sick by the king, symbolised the sacred authority of the monarch (Charles II touched 100 000; James VII and II spent more on this manifestation of Anglican sacred power than he did on promoting his own Catholicism through education). After 1688, none but the Stuarts continued the

Touch (Anne was the last reigning monarch to give it, though Charles Edward's brother Henry 'IX' continued its use until the end of the 18th century). The sacramental status of Anglican monarchy was damaged both by the overthrow of the Stuarts (legitimate heirs of every English and almost every Scottish royal house since the 9th century), and also through the accession of Protestant non-Anglicans, William and George I, who was a Lutheran. Of course the Stuarts were by this time Catholics: but they nonetheless remained attached to rites practised by Anglican sacramental monarchy, and continued to nominate bishops from the ranks of the Episcopal/Anglican clergy who remained loyal to them. In 1688-9, almost all Scottish Episcopalian priests (about 600) and a number of the bishops and clergy of the Church of England, including the Archbishop of Canterbury, refused to give allegiance to the new regime, thus beginning a century of the most severe split Anglicanism has yet faced. The size of this split has been variously estimated: but since the refusal to give allegiance meant the loss of any prospect of employment, it is important to remember that these clergy had many fellow-travellers who continued in the Church of England, including famous Jacobite figures such as Sacheverell and Atterbury, Bishop of Rochester. The Non-jurors were at the core of a presentation of Stuart kingship as an absent system of right which would return to provide messianic deliverance.

The sacred monarchy's absence altered the condition of the kingdom. The sacred king's association with the sun (found in the literature of both the Stuarts and the Bourbons) dated back to Roman times, possibly as far as Horace's great ode (*Odes* IV:v) on the returning light brought by the triumphant Augustus, who incidentally as Pontifex Maximus ('chief priest':a title now held by the Pope) after 12 BC, was himself a quasi-sacred figure. The king's absence was thus the absence of light from the land. Symbols of sacramental monarchy were important to those parts of the Anglican/Episcopal Church which supported the Stuarts. The martyrdom of Charles I, described by a later Anglican devotee in these terms :'St. Charles of England *Pray for us*..."Princely Pelican" despoiling thyself of thy substance, for the Church', led to a series of iconic representations: pictures and relics of the king are still found in churches. Similarly, the Revolution of 1688-9 led to passionate protest, as in this sermon from the Episcopal priest Professor James Garden, given in the New Church of Aberdeen in 1715:

> By it [the Revolution] the ancient Apostolick Form of Church Government was abolished and the true and Lawfull pastors of the

Church deprived and violently thrust from their offices, Houses and Livings, and exposed with their Families to Misery and want: the Right of the Church usurped by Schismatical Teachers, who have set up a Seperate [sic] Communion from the Catholick Church of Christ in all ages...For thes [sic] heinous Sins... the only natural and proper remedy [is]...the Restauration of his present.

Matie, James the 8th...

Many among the high church's supporters put their hopes in the Stuarts, and Jacobite failure led to the decline of high Anglicanism until its revival by the Oxford Movement in the 19th century (many of whose chief members were themselves sympathetic to the Jacobites). James was depicted as a sun, or seen as an exiled King David, driven abroad by the unrighteousness of his people. His return was awaited by Britannia, an image of Britain much strengthened under the Stuarts (Charles II first placed her on the coinage). Britannia herself could stand for the abandoned lady of the land mourning her absent king-lover, or the Blessed Virgin, mother of the Church which was in its turn the Bride of Christ: she had been depicted as the Virgin, 'Mary Dolorosa' weeping over the Church in a print of 1682, for example. Britannia could thus be politically, erotically and religiously idealised: an indeterminately idealised and yearning Britannia is seen on the 'Amor et Spes' (Love and Hope) medal minted for Charles Edward Stuart in the 1740s. The object of that love was made clear in the 'Look Love and Follow' medallion of Charles's bust which was produced at about the same time.

The sacred messianic approach was paralleled in the classical elements of Jacobite high culture, particularly the Brut myth, which claimed that

1. 'Amor et Spes' Britannia medal, produced in protest against the Treaty of Aix-la-Chapelle (1748).

Scottish National Portrait Gallery and the National Library of Scotland

Anglo-British monarchy had been founded by the grandson of Aeneas the Trojan, himself the apocryphal founder of the Roman state. Hence all legitimate monarchy was derived from Aeneas (this belief was not finally overthrown until well into the 18th century) and as the rightful rulers the Stuarts were likened to him. Virgil's great epic the *Aeneid* had implicitly compared Augustus to Aeneas, and so the Stuarts, already seen as Augusti in the poetry of John Dryden for example, inherited this image also (in the 18th century, there was a considerable struggle over such Augustanism between Jacobite and Hanoverian writers). Virgil's Fourth Eclogue, which predicts the coming of a messianic figure born of a virgin, has been taken to apply both to Astraea (the embodiment of justice and the golden age) and Augustus, and to Christ and Mary. James VIII and III's mother was Mary of Modena, and the comparison with Virgil had been made in *Britannia Rediviva*, the poem by Dryden which greeted James's birth. Hence the idea of messianic advent had strong roots in both sacred and classical Jacobite high culture, while the stories of the exile of Aeneas and fall of Troy appealed as suitable images for the plight of the Stuarts. Dryden's 1697 translation of the *Aeneid* is studded with Jacobite references, and the exiled king was frequently referred to as 'Aeneas', as in Robert Forbes' letter of 9 April 1743 to Oliphant of Gask which gives thanks for 'the kind providence of Heaven for so remarkably preserving AEneas & his two Sons' from an illness 'raging...on the other side of the water'. Captain Daniel, an Englishman who served in the '45 Rising, likewise describes Charles as a 'Trojan hero' and ends his memoir with a quotation equating the defeat of the Rising with the fall of Troy. The sufferings of the exiled king and the idea of his restoration to his kingdom are encapsulated in both classical and biblical terms in the 1708 medal by Norbert Roettier which depicts James's three kingdoms (England, Scotland and Ireland) surrounded by the ships which are to bring the exile home. The legend is 'Reddite' (Restore). Forty years later the return of his rights to the exile was still a central Jacobite theme, as evidenced in Dr William King's infamous Oxford speech of 1747, which called for the restoration ('Redeat') of Charles Edward as 'that great Genius of Britain': a messianic leader in classical dress.

Classical high cultural Jacobitism could be linked with the idea of James as a magical monarch and fertility king. Aeneas had taken a bough from a sacred oak tree in order to visit the underworld, and the oak was also strongly associated with the Stuart dynasty, most particularly Charles II, who famously escaped after the Battle of Worcester by hiding in one

2. 1750 Oak Society medal, minted in support of Charles Edward Stuart.

Scottish National Portrait Gallery and the National Library of Scotland

(the Royal Oak of the pub signs). In addition, the oak was strongly associated with the Druids and native folk culture, while the Christian Church was often depicted as a tree. When William came to power in 1688 (1689 in Scotland), medals struck in his honour showed a shattered and overthrown oak tree, symbol of the Stuart dynasty. Jacobite propagandists responded, as in the 1750 *'Revirescit'* (It flourishes) medal of the Royal Oak Society , which depicts a fresh sapling (Charles Edward) growing at the root of a withered oak. The renewed oak was an image of fertility, and the Jacobite claimant was depicted as a man in a tree, a kind of green man bringing the land back to life. Such fertility symbolism can be seen in 'The Agreable Contrast', where Charles Edward stands beside a tree in fuller blossom than does Cumberland in his butcher's apron. Flora MacDonald stands beside the Prince, and she remarks approvingly on the 'Long tail' of the suggestively phallic greyhound who accompanies him. By contrast, Cumberland's elephant has 'a pittefull tail', and Flora's full basket (not to mention her name) help to reinforce the symbolism of the fecund Charles and his sterile Hanoverian opponent.

Such imagery is found throughout the Jacobite high culture of Britain, including the Gaelic culture of Scotland and Ireland, where the belief that the just king had powers of restorative fertility was enduring. Gaelic writers repeatedly discuss the Stuarts in similar terms to their English-speaking counterparts. Iain MacLachlainn promises that 'The earth will yield crops without stint', while Alasdair MacMhaigstir Alasdair (Captain in the '45 and the Prince's Gaelic tutor) promises bright days and

THE AGREABLE CONTRAST·

Shews that a Greyhound is more agreable than an Elephant, & a Genteel personage
More agreably Pleasing than a Clumsey one, a Country Lass is better y.n a town trollop

3. 'The Agreable
Contrast', 1740s
Jacobite print.

Scottish National
Portrait Gallery

restored sunlight on the return of the king, and draws a striking parallel between James and Christ through the metaphor of the Eucharist:

> The health of King James Stewart,
>   Full gladly pass it round !
> But if within you fault is hidden
>   Soil not the holy cup.

Perhaps in recognition of this common culture, Episcopalians and Roman Catholics may have remained sympathetic to Gaelic while others in Scotland were trying to suppress it. In Ireland, where high church writers like Jonathan Swift seem to have been acquainted with Gaelic bardic culture, the *aisling* tradition presented a powerful image of the Stuart prince as heroic deliverer of an abandoned nation (Hibernia rather than Britannia, of course). For a poet like Eoghan Rua Ó Suilleabhain Charles Edward is 'the great Son of Glory'.

While sacred and classical aspects of high cultural Jacobitism found echoes in folk and popular culture, it was perhaps the fertility imagery of the magical monarch which appealed most to customary beliefs. Whether it is the case or not (as Daniel Defoe tells us) that 6,325 maypoles were erected in the five years after Charles II's Restoration in May 1660, both Charles and his nephew (James VIII and III, born on 10 June) symbolized the idea of the Stuarts as Spring monarchs, bringing

4. Jacobite print depicting Charles Edward as Highland hero.

Scottish National Portrait Gallery and the National Library of Scotland

light and life to the land. There were two major points of contact between popular celebration and the ideology of Jacobite high culture: traditional modes of patronage and the revelry of carnival, street theatre and the inn. Jacobite balladeers took advantage of popular carnival, just as poets, singers and the disaffected clergy relied on sympathetic gentry patronage.

Popular street theatre showed marked Jacobite tendencies by the early 18th century. The presence of disaffected groups from the upper ranks of society at such events has been well documented, but the events themselves remained in the control of the people, what Paul Monod (in his essay on 'Pierre's White Hat', see Bibliography) has called the 'improvised oral communication' of folk culture itself, as well as the printed ballads of a popular culture whose written texts interacted with the oral tradition of folk models. Street culture under Charles II had already seen a convergence between the interests of different classes, and this now intensified. Allusive codes revealed Jacobite sympathy publicly while rendering prosecution less likely, and to achieve this end, well-known folk songs and motifs were adapted for Jacobite use. An example of this is the 'Bonnie Highland Laddie' song-cycle, where the motif of a rough, poor Highlander seducing a Lowland gentlewoman

5. Anti-Jacobite print of Charles Edward as 'Pied Piper' figure.

Scottish National Portrait Gallery and the National Library of Scotland

becomes a celebration of Charles Edward Stuart. The Highlander is now
Prince Charles; his poverty becomes patriotic honesty (he has not been
'bought and sold for English gold'), and the seduction becomes a
renewing fertility which liberates the beloved woman (in this case,
Scotland) from the slavery of Hanoverian Union into a realm of liberated
sexual glee. From the threatening outsider of the folksong, the
Highlander becomes the Jacobite patriot: and Highland dress
symbolizes such patriotism, irrespective of cultural background: hence
Charles Edward put his *Lowland* troops in Highland garb in 1745. The

potency of the image of Charles as Highlander was recognized both by the Jacobites and the Hanoverians who here portray him as a Pied Piper-like seducer. On occasion (especially after dressing as a woman in the Betty Burke episode), Charles was identified not just as the land's lover but as the female personification of the land itself: hence *perhaps* he is shown as a woman on Jacobite drinking-glasses (six of which survive). Hanoverian propaganda took the episode as an excuse to deride Charles's masculinity.

Music was also a central part of popular Jacobite celebration. Setting pro-Stuart verses to a familiar air was a common device: thus in mixed company, or when danger threatened, the fiddler or piper could play a tune that sympathizers could recognize, but which it would be difficult for the authorities to take action against (that they often did take such action when they could is evidenced in the number of 'seditious words' prosecutions). Indeed, even more overtly Jacobite tunes were not exactly direct treasonable statements, as is perhaps recalled in 'The Piper of Dundee':

> He play'd 'The Welcome owre the Main',
> And, 'Ye'se be fou and I'se be fain',
> And 'Auld Stuarts back again',
>> Wi' muckle mirth and glee...

> And wisnae he a roguie,
> A roguie, a roguie,
> And wisnae he a roguie,
>> The Piper o' Dundee ?

Cultural expressions of sympathy for the Stuart cause were widespread, and not only in Scotland. The inn was a central meeting-place for Jacobite folk/popular culture, particularly in safe areas. Broadsides were pasted up there in continuation of a longstanding tradition of alehouse ballad-hawking, while the place of women in transmitting Jacobite traditions may reflect their centrality in the wider world of folk culture. Such traditions could be enduring. In the five years from George I's coronation (itself more than a quarter of a century after the deposition of James VII and II), there were Jacobite disturbances in 57 English and Welsh towns, and images of the Hanoverians were publicly exhibited and defiled in English popular celebration until several years after the '45. The song-culture of Jacobitism was integrated into the Risings themselves: not only did balladeers march with the Stuart forces in both

1715 and 1745, but Jacobite songs still sung seem to date from these occasions, as in the case of 'Little ken ye wha's coming' ('The Chevalier's Muster-Roll'), a copy of which is dated 12 November 1715 with the comment 'played by the Highland piper when the army was in England'. A Highland piper playing a song written in Scots is an apt symbol of the cross-class and cross-community values found in Jacobite culture. As has been pointed out, the Gaeltacht shows the same signs of high and folk cultural interchange as are found outside it.

Jacobitism was a complex culture of protest against the overthrow of a sacred monarchy in a world where religion was far more important than it seems now. It was also the voice of opposition to the rapid development of the British state which followed the exile of the Stuarts: the central nationalist voice in both Scotland and Ireland for much of the 18th century. As a movement, it represented far more than the monarchs whose cause it supported. Its legacies are with us yet, and some of the questions it asked have never been answered. Through its cultural life, we can see into a lost world far more diverse and interesting than can be provided by Bonnie Prince Charlie as he appears today.

Bibliography

John Lorne Campbell, (ed.), *Highland Songs of the Forty-Five*, Edinburgh, 1984 (1933).

Eveline Cruickshanks and Jeremy Black (eds.), *The Jacobite Challenge,* Edinburgh, 1988.

William Donaldson, *The Jacobite Song*, Aberdeen, 1988.

Madge Dresser, 'Britannia', in volume 3 of Samuel Raphael (ed.), *Patriotism*, 3 vols., London, 1991.

William Gillies, 'Gaelic Songs of the 'Forty-Five', *Scottish Studies* 30, 1991, pp19-58.

Frank McLynn, *The Jacobites,* London, 1985; *Charles Edward Stuart* ,London, 1988; *Crime and Punishment in Eighteenth-Century England,* London, 1989.

Roger Mason, 'Scotching the Brut: Politics, History and National Myth in Sixteenth-Century Britain', in Mason (ed.), *Scotland and England 1286-1815*, Edinburgh, 1987.

Paul Monod, *Jacobitism and the English People,* Cambridge, 1989; 'Pierre's White Hat' in Eveline Cruickshanks (ed.), *By Force or By Default?* Edinburgh, 1989.

Murray G H Pittock, *The Invention of Scotland: The Stuart Myth and the Scottish Identity, 1638 to the Present,* London and New York, 1991.

Nicholas Rogers, *Whigs and Cities,* Oxford, 1989.

Daniel Szechi, *The Jacobites,* Manchester, 1994.

Noel Woolf, *The Medallic Record of the Scottish Jacobite Movement,* London, 1988.

Chapter Seven

SYMBOLS
AND SENTIMENT:
JACOBITE GLASS

Brian J. R. Blench

IT is now almost a hundred years since the publication of Albert Hartshorne's *Old English Glasses* – 'the history of a subject never before undertaken for England'.[1] The volume laid the foundation of the academic study of British glass and coincidentally made its collecting equally acceptable, at the same time fuelling an interest in Jacobite glass in particular by devoting a whole chapter to these 'historical relics of a hapless cause'. In the intervening years scholars and collectors have corrected, added to and refined Hartshorne's chronology of the development of British glass as a whole while continuing to debate the dating, origins and significance of those pieces apparently devoted to the Jacobite cause. While most advances in our knowledge of glass history are firmly rooted in contemporary documentary sources – bills, letters, account books, advertisements, and company sales catalogues – there is hardly any direct evidence of this kind to explain any of the puzzles and mysteries which surround Jacobite glass. Collectors and historians have relied on conjecture, imagination or assertion in their attempts to answer questions as to why, when, where and by whom the glasses were made and to explain the symbols with which they are decorated. For it is only in their decoration that they are distinguished from the innumerable surviving examples of the golden age of British glass-making. Emblems and inscriptions associated with the 'Cause' are found on all standard 18th century glass forms – it has been their interpretation which has provided the battleground.

The reasons for the popularity of Jacobite glasses among collectors are not hard to find. They are normally of good quality glass, elegant in form, attractively decorated and, perhaps above all, associated with one of the most dramatic and romantic periods of Anglo-Scottish history – the final demise of the Stuart cause. The resurgence of interest in Jacobite studies in the last twenty years has had a corollary in a new approach to the study of the glasses not as secondary sources but as primary sources in themselves as indicators of the breadth of sympathy for the movement, particularly in the years surrounding 1745. Detailed examination of nearly 500 specimens by Dr G B Seddon has provided several clues to the solution of many of the problems which have occupied glass historians in the past.[2]

The decoration of 18th century glasses which distinguishes them as Jacobite is, with the exception of a handful of portrait glasses (see p 91–2), either diamond-point or copper-wheel engraving – there are no examples recorded to date of stipple engraving where the image is produced by striking a diamond or steel point against the glass to make a mass of tiny dots. In diamond-point engraving the surface of the glass is scratched with a hand-held diamond pointed tool. A simple technique in that it requires little equipment, it has been practised since Roman times and in England certainly since the late 16th century. Considerable skill is however needed to achieve a high quality effect. Copper-wheel engraving, in contrast, requires both long training and a wide range of equipment.

The glass is engraved by an abrasive suspended in an oily medium which is brought into contact with the glass surface by means of a copper wheel mounted on a revolving spindle. This is bench mounted and in the 18th century was powered by a foot operated mechanism. The cut made when the glass is brought into contact with the wheel depends on its size, both diameter and thickness. Engravers might employ up to one hundred different wheels to achieve the wide variety of effects which make wheel engraving so variable. The technique only appears to have reached England from the continent of Europe around 1700 but did not really become established till the 1740s – a fact which has considerable bearing on the study of Jacobite glass.

The most immediately recognisable group of Jacobite glasses are the 'Amen' glasses. Though not the rarest type, some thirty-five are known to have survived, they are certainly the most expensive for the modern collector.[3] All have certain common features; they are all diamond-point engraved and have part, usually two or more verses of, or variations on the Jacobite anthem:

God save the King, I pray
God bliss the King, I pray
God save the King
Send him victorious
Happy and glorious
Soon to reign over us,
God save the King

God Bliss the Prince of Wales,
The true-born Prince of Wales,
Sent us by Thee.
Grant us one favour more,
The King for to restore,
As thou hast done before,
The familie.

God save the Church, I pray,
God bliss the Church I pray,
Pure to remain.
Against all heresie,
And Whig's hipocrasie,
Who strive maliciouslie,
Her to defame.

God bless the subjects all,
And save both great and small
In every station.
That will bring home the King,
Who hath best right to reign,
It is the only thing,
Can save the Nation.

If there were any doubt about which king is concerned the glasses all feature the cypher JR (Jacobus Rex) both direct and reversed above a small figure 8. Sometimes the 8 is larger and is incorporated in the cypher. The 'Old Pretender' would have been James VIII of Scotland, and III of England. The second verse refers to his legitimacy though earlier scholars used this to suggest that the glasses were made soon after 1720 to celebrate the birth of Charles Edward Stuart.

Some glasses have additional toasts 'To His Royal Highness Prince Henry', 'To the Increase of the Royal Family', or to the Jacobite families

1. The Erskine of Cardross II 'Amen' glass.

Glasgow Museums

that owned them as in 'Prosperity to the Family of Traquair', or even to individuals. One, for example, carries an inscription on the foot to 'Donald MacLeod of Gaultergil in the Isle of Skye. The Faithful Palinurus. Aet 69 Anno 1747'.

Another even has a more precise wish:

> Send him soon home   To Holyrood House
> And that no Sooner   Than I do wish
> Vive La Roi

Some early scholars suggested that these glasses had been engraved in France though with little or no supporting evidence. Recent close examination of the calligraphy suggests that they are the work of one engraver whose standard of proficiency improved with practice. The earliest dated example is from 1743 and the latest 1749 so it seems likely that all were produced between 1740 and 1750. One feature of interest which has relevance to the later discussion of the symbols on wheel-engraved Jacobite glasses is that almost one-third of the glasses have the additional dedication to Prince Henry (see p 94).[4]

Another very much smaller group of glasses about whose purpose there can be no confusion are the nine wine glasses decorated in coloured enamels with a portrait of Prince Charles Edward Stuart in tartan dress. Despite or perhaps even because of their rarity they have attracted less attention from the collectors than the 'Amen' series.

All have opaque-twist stems, indicating a later date of production but there the similarity ends. Three rather sketchily painted in red, white and blue colours, have a half-length portrait of the prince wearing the tartan he is said to have adopted before his entry into Manchester, 29 November 1745.

A contemporary account stated that:

> 'The Prince entered at two in the afternoon walking in the midst of a select band of Highlanders; his dress a light tartan plaid, belted with a blue sash, a gray wig, and a blue velvet bonnet, topped by a rose of white ribbons, the badge of his house'.[5]

Five other glasses in the series are better executed in white, red, black, blue, yellow and green. One of these, now in the Royal Museums of Scotland, presented by Miss Sylvia Steuart, has a very interesting

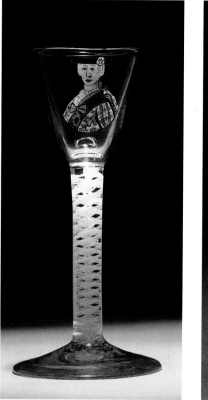

provenance. It is reputed to be one of a group of 'six glasses made, having upon them a coloured representation of the Prince, for drinking his health'[6] presented by Thomas Erskine, later 9th Earl of Kellie, to a group of staunch Jacobites who met annually at Mr Steuart's house, Clelands Gardens, Edinburgh, the last meeting of which was held on 31 December 1787 and was attended by Robert Burns.[7]

Two other glasses are similar in style and quality of painting to this but are rather larger and seem unlikely to be part of the original six. Two further glasses[8] have portraits closer in style to the three-coloured versions, while a final unique glass (see illustration 3), again in only three colours, is different in that the portrait in this instance is only head and shoulders. The three-coloured glasses are generally assumed to be earlier than the polychrome examples which are thought to date from about 1775.[9]

Well over ninety per cent of the recorded Jacobite glasses are copper wheel engraved with a variety of motifs and inscriptions whose precise

4. Waterbowl engraved with seven-petalled rose and half-open bud on a stem with five leaves. On the reverse is a moth. c 1780

Drambuie Collection

explanation has been the subject of much discussion by historians and collectors. The principal motif is usually a rose, normally six-petalled though seven and eight-petalled varieties are not uncommon. The five-petalled rose, like the Tudor rose, is rare and may merely be attributable to poor engraving. The rose is usually accompanied by a thorned stem which may branch to carry one or two buds. If there is only one bud it is closed and on the right of the flower when viewed. If there are two buds the second bud is open and on the left of the flower. When there is only a single bud the plant normally has five accompanying leaves, four if there are two buds. The number of elements therefore usually adds up to seven referring no doubt to James VII of Scotland and II of England.

The rose had long been a badge of the Stuart dynasty – perhaps as far back as David II who is reputed to have chosen it as his badge at a tournament at Windsor Castle while a prisoner after the Battle of Neville's Cross in 1346.[10] Certainly by the beginning of the 18th century, the white rose was closely associated with the Stuart cause, being worn especially on 10 June, the birthday of James VIII and III, the Old Pretender. However, the precise interpretation of the flower and buds and what or who they represent has been a source of constant discussion. The arguments often developed a circular form by dating glasses from their supposed symbolism and then using this dating to reinforce the symbolism.

The main theories may be tabulated for convenience.

| Author | Interpretation | | |
	Rose	Closed Bud	Open Bud
pre 1940	James VII	James VIII	Charles Edward
Steevenson 1 bud	James VIII	Charles Edward	
2 bud	James VIII	Henry Benedict	Charles Edward
Horridge	Triple crown	James VIII	Charles Edward
Barrington Haynes 1 bud	Crown of England	James VIII	
2 bud	Crown of England	Charles Edward	James VIII
Seddon	James VII	Charles Edward	Henry Benedict

Most of the earlier theories depended on the assumption that the motifs followed a chronological pattern of a rose with a single bud, then double bud, then again a single bud. The earlier single bud represented Prince Charles, the two buds appearing with Prince Henry's coming of age, and reverting to a single bud on his elevation to the cardinalate in 1747. It is now evident that the rose with a single bud appears throughout the whole Jacobite period.[11]

Other motifs present fewer problems. The oakleaf, for example, had long been a Stuart clan emblem, reputedly worn in their bonnets when going to battle.[12] Its significance was

5. Wine glass engraved with six-petalled rose, half-open bud and five leaves.
c 1750

Drambuie Collection

6. Decanter engraved with eight-petalled rose, three quarter and half-open buds and seven leaves. On the reverse oak leaves, star and compass and the inscription 'FIAT'.

Drambuie Collection

reinforced by Charles II's hiding in the Boscobel oak after the Battle of Worcester in 1651 and his wearing a sprig of oak-leaves on his return to London on Oak Apple Day, 29 May 1660. A related symbol is the representation of a stricken oak with a vigorous sapling close by anticipating the renewal of the Stuart monarchy. (See Chapter six for more on symbolism of motifs.)

The presence of a thistle on many glasses is an equally indisputable reference to the national emblem of Scotland which had been in use since the time of James III of Scotland. The Order of the Thistle had been reinstituted in 1687 and James VIII and III had invested Prince Charles in infancy.

Two motifs carry more obvious personal reference to Prince Charles Edward – a star and the feathers. On the night of his birth a new star was reported and generally accepted as a good omen – a symbol of hope.

The normal form on the glasses is that of six-pointed star. The ostrich feathers in a group of three sometimes arising from a crown is a reference to Prince Charles as heir apparent, Prince of Wales. They are frequently engraved on the underside of the foot of the glass.

Another symbol whose significance is certainly not fully understood is that of the compass rose frequently associated with the star. Together they feature on decanters. The indicator on the compass usually points to 45° and is aligned with the star. It has been suggested that this may indicate 'The King over the water' but if the star symbolizes Charles Edward it would be inappropriate before 1766, the year of the Old Pretender's death. If however it is regarded as a nautical compass, a true course dead ahead would be to the north-west ie Scotland, the direction from which Charles Edward was coming or had come.

Another group of symbols which appear, along with others of a more obvious interpretation, are bees, butterflies and moths. It is frequently difficult to distinguish the latter two perhaps because the engravers themselves may have had the same problems. Their meanings are generally accepted, the bee signifying loyalty, the butterfly the return of the soul. Some glasses have grubs which may be a reference to an old Scottish belief that the soul of a dead exiled Scot returns to his native land by an underground route. Alternatively all may be merely decorative elements of the basically floral naturalistic design.

7. Wine glass with engraved portrait.

Glasgow Museums

Other flowers which appear on Jacobite glasses would appear to be chosen for their traditional symbolic meaning. These include Daffodils (hope, as yet unfulfilled), Honeysuckle (fidelity), Lily of the

Valley (return to happiness), Sunflower (unswerving loyalty), Forget-me-nots, and Carnation (coronation). On occasion these flowers along with the rose and thistle form a decorative border to the bowl of the glass – the so-called disguised Jacobite glasses. Some flowered glasses appear to have been produced in sets where the initial letters of the plants can be arranged in an appropriate acrostic.[13]

The final group of engraved glasses bear a portrait of Charles Edward: they are of three types. A few are merely of the head in profile and are probably based on medals issued in 1745 or 1752. The largest number depict Charles in tartan dress, with bonnet and cockade as on the enamelled glasses. It is likely that the source for these is a composite of various paintings or engravings of the prince.

The third group, again in profile, show the prince wearing the Order of the Garter on the wrong breast and have been a source of much discussion. Various theories have been advanced, usually with a numismatic ground or blaming incompetent foreign engravers. However it has recently been shown that none of these bear the inscription normally associated with the portrait glasses and that they were probably meant to be held with the portrait away from the drinker thus reversing the figure.

A final feature of many glasses is an inscription, the vast majority of which are Latin. This can hardly have been an attempt to hide their political significance as Latin as well as a knowledge of classical literature would have been assumed on the part of any educated person. Jacobite glasses are quasi-heraldic and Latin is used extensively in heraldry.

The motto most commonly associated with the portrait glasses AUDENTIOR IBO is a quotation from the sixth book of Virgil's *Aeneid* where Aeneas is encouraged by the Sybil to act with greater daring. By the alteration of one of the letters in the injunction 'ito' to 'ibo' the Jacobite meaning is created; 'I shall go more boldly'.[14] Another motto associated with a portrait HIC VIR HIC EST – 'this is the man, this is he' again derives from the *Aeneid* where Aeneas is permitted to see the future consequences of his flight from Troy. The golden age of Rome under Augustus Caesar, who is introduced with these words, indicates the coming of a similar golden age to Scotland. A last quotation from the same source, TURNO TEMPUS ERIT – 'for Turnus there shall be a time' was once interpreted to mean that there would be a time for Charles Edward, but a closer examination of the Latin context suggests that Turnus who was killed by Aeneas represents the Duke of Cumberland. In other words the Hanoverian victory at Culloden might be reversed.

Other inscriptions are simpler. REVIRESCIT, usually associated with the stricken oak motif, means 'it grows green again'. REDEAT – 'may he return', REDDITE – 'restore', REDI – 'return', all are powerful in their simplicity and use of the imperative. Yet others by their terseness are equally inspiring AB OBICE MAJOR –

8. *Wine glass engraved with six-petalled rose, three quarter and half-open buds, stem with two leaves and a star.*

Inscribed 'FIAT' and 'TURNO TEMPUS ERIT' on bowl and 'REDEAT' on foot.

Drambuie Collection

'greater from the check' presumably the 'check' of Culloden; CAELUM NON ANIMUM MUTANT QUI TRANS MARE CURRUNT – 'they change clime not heart who speed across the sea'; COGNOSCUNT ME MEI – 'my own recognise me'; FLOREAT – 'may it flourish'; PREMIUM VIRTUTIS – 'reward of valour'; PRO PATRIA – 'for the sake of the country'; and REDDAS INCOLUMEM – 'restore unharmed'. The most frequently encountered inscription however is the simple FIAT – 'may it come to pass'. Fiat is also the equivalent of 'Amen' – 'may it be so'.[15] At one time this was thought to be the password of the most well known of the Jacobite clubs – The Cycle of the White Rose[16] – but the frequency with which it appears makes this unlikely. It is however not unlikely that many of the glasses were used by clubs and organisations with Jacobite sympathies – over one hundred and fifty have been recorded, nearly all in England and Wales. Few lasted for long periods, many declined into social or sporting clubs as the likelihood of the Stuart restoration declined. Some may indeed never have had any serious political purpose but only have included known sympathizers in the membership as did the bawdy 'Beggars Benison of Anstruther'.[17]

9. Wine glass engraved with six-petalled rose, three quarter and half-open buds and stem with four leaves.

Inscribed 'REDI', between two engraved oak leaves, on foot.

Glasgow Museums

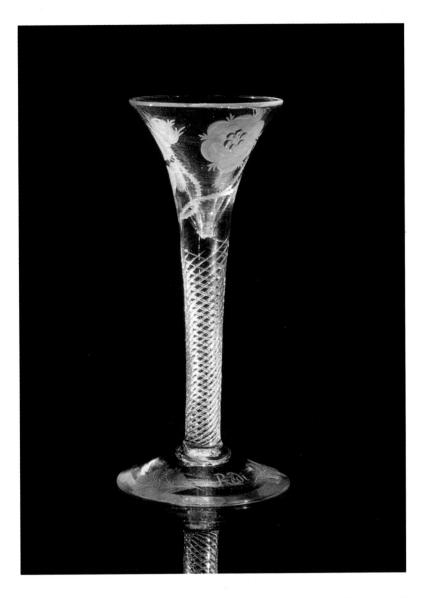

For many years it was asserted that most Jacobite glasses, because of their forms and the size of the bowl, had been produced after the introduction of the Excise Act of 1745 which imposed heavy duty on glass. Numismatic evidence for the origin of the symbols and mottos was used to support this[18] and so it was thought that most Jacobite glass was made and decorated after about 1750. More recent studies, based on a detailed study of the engraving and the form of glasses used suggests that a much greater number than was thought were probably engraved before, during and after the year of the Rebellion, and probably in London. Dr Seddon has been able to 'identify' the hand of some nine individual craftsmen, though as yet they remain anonymous.[19]

The making and decorating of Jacobite glass remains still something of a mystery, however these 'frail relics' do indicate by their survival the extent of sympathy for the Stuart cause even if when the time came to take action many supporters seem to have been content merely to drink to the 'King over the water'.

Notes

1. Hartshorne, 1897.

2. I would like to acknowledge the generosity of Dr Seddon in allowing me access to the typescript of his book *The Jacobites and their Drinking Glasses* in preparation of this chapter.

3. A recent example to appear on the market, the Spottiswoode 'Amen' glass realised £66,000 at Sotheby's in April 1991. It is now in the Drambuie Collection.

4. For a full listing and discussion of 'Amen' glasses see Charleston and Seddon, 1986, and Seddon *op cit.*

5. Quoted in R Chambers, 1869, p185. Grant R Francis (1926) attributes the description to a Mr Andrews and quotes more extensively – '...blue velvet bonnet which seems to have been his covering throughout the whole campaign, was now adorned in the centre of the top with a white rose to distinguish him from his officers, all of whom wore their cockades on one side.' p.178.

6. Registration number MEN 94. For a fuller account of this and other enamelled glasses see Churchill Glass Notes, 1956, S Cottle, 'The Other Beilbys: British enamelled glass of the eighteenth century', *Apollo*, October 1986, pp315-27, and J Steuart. At the back of St James's Square. *Book of the Old Edinburgh Club*, Vol. 2, 1909, pp167–75.

7. Burns's poem *'Afar the illustrious Exile roams'*, was written for this occassion.

8. One in the Drambuie Collection, the other sold recently at Phillips, London, 14 September 1994, now in a private collection.

9. This group of glasses is currently the subject of study by the author.

10. This was perhaps reinforced by the fact that several of Scotland's kings and queens had received the Papal gift of a Golden Rose, see C J Burnet and C J Tabraham, *The Honours of Scotland*, Historic Scotland, Edinburgh, 1993.

11. For fuller discussion of the symbolism of the rose and buds see M Steevenson, (various), W Horridge, 1944, E Barrington Haynes, 1959, Grant R Francis, 1926 and G B Seddon, *op cit*.

12. There remains some dispute about the traditional association of certain clans with certain plants, see F Adam, 1970.

13. For further discussion of such glasses see J M Bacon, 1942 and the same author in *Country Life*, September 12, 1947, p523.

14. 'Ito' is the imperative 'go', while 'ibo' is the future tense 'I shall go'.

15. For a fuller discussion of the Latin mottos see F J Lelièvre, 1986.

16. See Grant R Francis, 1933.

17. *Records of the most ancient and puissant order of the Beggar's Benison and Merryland, Anstruther.* Anstruther, privately printed 1892. Reprinted Paul Harris Publishing, Edinburgh, 1982.

18. See Grant R Francis, 1925 and 1926.

19. Seddon, *op cit*.

Selected Bibliography

Frank Adam, Revised Sir Thomas Innes of Learney, *The Clans, Septs, and Regiments of the Scottish Highlands*, 8th Edn, Johnston and Bacon, Stirling, 1984.

John M Bacon, Notes on Jacobite Glass, *Glass Circle Paper No 30*, 1942.

Percy Bate, *English Table Glass*, Charles Scribner's Sons, New York, 1905.

L M Bickerton, *Eighteenth Century English Drinking Glasses, an illustrated guide*, Antique Collectors' Club, Woodbridge, 1986.

Joseph Bles, *Rare English Glasses of the 17th and 18th Centuries*, Houghton Mifflin Co, Boston, 1925.

Francis Buckley, *History of Old English Glass*, Benn, London, 1925.

R Chambers, *History of the Rebellion of 1745–46*, 7th Edn, W R Chambers, London and Edinburgh, 1869.

R J Charleston and G Seddon, 'Amen' Glasses, *The Glass Circle*, 5, London, 1986.

Arthur Churchill, Ltd. *Glass Notes*, Nos 7–16, London, 1947–56.

J A Fleming, *Scottish and Jacobite Glass*, Reprint, EP Publishing Ltd. East Ardsley, 1977.

Grant R Francis, Jacobite Drinking Glasses, *British Numismatic Journal*, Vol. XVI, 1925.

Grant R Francis, *Old English Drinking Glasses, their chronology and sequence*, Herbert Jenkins, London, 1926.

Grant R Francis, *Romance of the White Rose*, J. Murray, London, 1933.

Albert Hartshorne, *Old English Glasses*, Edward Arnold, London, 1897.

E Barrington Haynes, *Glass Through the Ages*, Penguin, Harmandsworth, 1959.

W Horridge, and E B Haynes, The Amen Glasses, *Connoisseur*, September 1942.

W Horridge, The Rose and Emblems on Jacobite Drinking Glasses, *Glass Circle Paper, No 56*, 1944.

G Bernard Hughes, *English, Scottish, and Irish Table Glass*, Lutterworth, London, 1956.

F J Lelièvre, Jacobite Glasses and their Inscriptions, *The Glass Circle*, 5, 1986, London.

J Sydney Lewis, *Old Glass and how to Collect it*, T Werner Laurie, London, 1928.

R A Robertson, *Chats on Old Glass*, rev edn Dover, New York, 1969.

Geoffrey B Seddon, The Jacobite Engravers, *The Glass Circle*, 3, London, 1979.

Geoffrey B Seddon, *The Jacobites and their Drinking Glasses*, Antique Collectors' Club, Woodbridge, 1995.

Muriel Steevenson, Jacobite Clubs, *Glass Circle Paper No 7*, 1939.

Muriel Steevenson, 'Amen' and 'Fiat', *Glass Circle Paper No 11*, 1940.

Muriel Steevenson, Jacobite Emblems, The Rose, *Glass Circle Paper No 12*, 1940.

Muriel Steevenson, More Emblems on Jacobite Glass, *Glass Circle Paper No 13*, 1940.

Muriel Steevenson, Some Jacobite Clubs, *Glass Circle Papers Nos 59, 60, 61*, all 1945.

Muriel Steevenson, Pruning the Jacobite Rose, *Glass Circle Paper, No 144*, 1966.

Chapter Eight

THE AFTERMATH OF
THE '45

Allan I. Macinnes

THE defeat of the Jacobite forces at Culloden on 16 April 1746, not only signalled the end of civil war and rebellion, but ushered in a period of indiscriminate repression within Scottish Gaeldom by the forces loyal to the Whig government. The immediate aftermath of the '45 was marked by genocidal clearance verging on ethnic cleansing; by banditry as a form of social protest; and by cultural alienation as chiefs and leading gentry abandoned their traditional obligations as protectors and patrons in pursuit of their commercial aspirations as proprietors. At the same time, because the clans had been the Scottish bedrock of the Jacobite cause since its foundation in 1689, the Whig government embarked upon a legislative as well as a military offensive to eradicate all cultural vestiges of clanship that were inconsistent with the advance of the British Empire. Property, progress and Protestantism were to become the watchwords for the civilisation, that is the assimilation of the Gaels as serviceable, industrious and dutiful subjects of the triumphalist, Whig regime of George II. Analogy can be drawn between the Jacobite clans and the Southern Confederacy during the American civil war. The fate of the Jacobites, like the Confederates one hundred and twenty years later, has attracted a romantic sentimentality; their respective sides in the civil wars had the better songs. More pertinently, the brutal suppression of both causes presaged the respective emergence of Britain and the United States as world powers.

Considerably greater numbers had deserted from than had been recruited to the Jacobite ranks during the unseasonable march from

Scotland into England in the winter of 1745. Nonetheless, the advance as far as Derby of a predominantly Highland army reputedly addicted to plunder and depredation had been depicted contemporaneously as the monstrous progress of a barbarous people whose ostensible, if surprising, closeness to London had sent tremendous convulsions throughout the British establishment. Moreover, some clans were actively engaged in their fourth Jacobite rebellion even though their chiefs and gentry since the time of Queen Anne had accepted gratuities – ranging from £100 to £500 annually – to accept the Treaty of Union of 1707 and the Hanoverian Succession in 1714. As the rival armies manoeuvred for the showdown at Culloden, the Whig military command described their opponents no longer as rebels and disturbers of the repose of Great Britain, but as cannibals. The commander of the government forces was William, Duke of Cumberland, who had been obliged to withdraw from the continental campaign against the French after Jacobite successes in Scotland had threatened political stability in England. The Whig establishment, particularly in England, exhorted Cumberland to make a final resolution of a damnable rebellion.

For their part, the Jacobite forces in the weeks before Culloden, already alarmed by Cumberland's manifest difficulties in maintaining martial law as his troops moved through north-east Scotland, were particularly apprehensive of the licence to dispense summary justice afforded to the Campbells among the clan contingents fighting for the Whigs. The intent of the government forces to inflict salutary and lasting punishment was bolstered by a polemical campaign in which Jacobites were castigated as slaves who were beyond the pale of civilised society. Leagued with the enemies of mankind, their extirpation was not only wished for, but in the case of the clans, opportune. The polemical onslaught against the rebels led to the deliberate perpetration of disinformation throughout the Empire. Thus, the *Virginia Gazette of Williamsburg*, which generally reported events two months after their occurrence, accompanied its report of Cumberland's victory with a reprint of an order reputedly written on the eve of Culloden by Lord George Murray, ordering the Jacobite forces to offer no quarter to the enemy. The letter, which did not feature in the first official reports of the battle that reached London on 23 April, subsequently surfaced as adverse publicity emerged about the severity of repression after Culloden. The letter was repudiated by the Jacobite commanders who, like Lord George, had been all but sidelined by Charles Edward Stuart prior to Culloden.

1. John Campbell of
the Bank by William
Mosman.

Campbell became
cashier of the Royal
Bank of Scotland in
1745 and he was a
factor to the
Campbell Earl of
Breadalbane.

The painting is
dated 1749 and he is
shown wearing
tartan despite its
proscription after
Culloden.

Royal Bank of
Scotland

Press reports that no quarter was given on either side were followed up by accounts of the aftermath of battle in which it was attested that it was extremely difficult to distinguish such of the common Highlanders that were in arms from those that threw their weapons away. Yet, their armed state was immaterial to the exaction of reprisals. Nothing but their own pertinacity and duplicity towards compliance with the Whig government was held to have occasioned their destruction. Indeed, Cumberland was reported as being best pleased when he found Highlanders denying having had any hand in the battle. Reports that the Whig troops were generally exasperated by the treatment meted out to those of their number they found almost naked and eaten up with vermin in dungeons at Inverness were issued to justify, not explain, the severe treatment and little quarter offered to the Jacobite forces already routed at Culloden. In like manner, the Whig government periodically issued reports in the eighteen months following Culloden of barbarous acts committed by Jacobite clans as far back as 1716 that had gone unpunished and, by 1749, was belatedly collating denials of excessive brutality and other atrocities against Jacobite prisoners.

The clear intent of the Whig commanders by Culloden, was to inflict such a crushing defeat on the Jacobite clans that they would remember it for generations. Cumberland was particularly intent on demonstrating that they could retire to no mountain so barren or so remote that he could not personally root them out. Indeed, he was convinced that the Jacobite rebellious principle was so rooted in the mind of the Scottish nation that a whole generation of clansmen must be pretty well

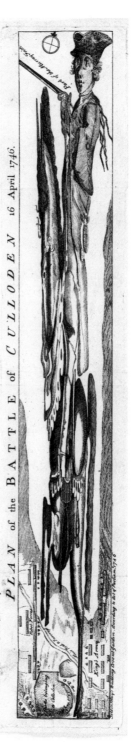

PLAN of the BATTLE of CULLODEN 16 April 1746.

2. *Plan of the Battle of Culloden, 16 April 1746. It also contains an anamorphic portrait of the Duke of Cumberland.*

The Hunterian Art Gallery

worn out before the country would be quiet. In making little effort to distinguish between rebellious Scots and Jacobite clansmen, Cumberland was prepared to implement the prevalent Scotophobia that predominated within government circles. Such Scotophobia has been excused on grounds of repeated rebellions from Scotland against the British state and the generally venal behaviour of Scottish politicians in seeking offices of place and profit from whatever ministry, Whig or even Tory, that was in power since the Union of Parliaments in 1707. Such a defence for political exasperation, however, cannot condone the atrocities perpetrated in the immediate aftermath of Culloden which moreover were carried on indiscriminately as a wanton campaign of genocide for almost twelve months after the battle.

Having instigated and encouraged genocide, Cumberland largely left the unsavoury task to such enthusiastic underlings as his compatriots William Anne Keppel, second Earl of Albemarle and Lieutenant-Colonel Edward Cornwallis who commanded psychotic Lowlanders like Major Lockhart and Captain Caroline Scott to run amok on land while Captain John Fergusson wreaked havoc by sea. Even Gaels such as Captain George Munro of Culcairn in Easter Ross and Captain Alexander Grant of Knockando in Strathspey set about this desperate task with a perverted will. The one notably restraining influence within the Whig military command was John Campbell, fourth Earl of Loudoun. Having been constantly on the defensive in seeking to contain the Jacobite clans within Scotland and having been driven from Inverness in the month before Culloden, he was under persistent political surveillance for his less than glorious contribution to the Whig victory. Nonetheless, his temperate and accommodating behaviour in seeking to encourage Jacobites to surrender their arms without recourse to unnecessary severity stood in marked contrast to other officers who glorified in clearing out Jacobite neighbourhoods around the garrisons at Inverness, Ruthven-in-Badenoch, Bernera in Glenelg, Fort Augustus and Fort William where women offering succour to wounded or starving prisoners were in particular danger of being strip searched and raped. In the process of clearing, those found in arms were peremptorily put to death. The houses of those who absconded in fear of draconian punishment were plundered and burned, their cattle driven away and their ploughs and other farming implements, boats and fishing tackle destroyed.

The extensive Loudoun papers on the campaign and its aftermath afford striking corroboration for the excessive reprisals meted out by government forces which have hitherto been publicised largely through the testimony of Jacobite victims and sympathisers, most notably *The Lyon in Mourning*, purposefully collated through the unstinting endeavours of Robert Forbes, Bishop of Ross and Caithness, from his release from prison in the month following Culloden until his death in 1775. Forbes and his fellow non-jurors – Episcopalians who refused to accept the Hanoverian succession – formed the bulk of Jacobite supporters in the Highlands as in the north-east. Their meeting-houses became prime targets for government forces as the penal laws were applied even more rigorously against non-jurors than against the Roman Catholics who shared the same faith as the exiled royal house of Stuart.

No reliable figures can be placed on the victims of genocide. Nonetheless, whole communities in the areas of Jacobite recruitment were terrorised by forced quartering and inquisitorial proceedings to establish which landowners, tenants, labourers and servants were at home during the '45 and which were out and liable to punitive reprisals. In such a climate of terror, informing became a growth. The body count in the sixteen months after Culloden, greatly supplemented the number of Jacobites, around 3000, slaughtered during and after the battle. Due process of law was ostensibly applied to no more than 2500 Jacobite prisoners who were shipped to England to face show-trials after prolonged incarceration in Carlisle, York and London. The prime issue to be determined in these trials, where one prisoner was arraigned as the representative of his cell block, was not of guilt but of final destination. The Jacobite rank and file sentenced to penal servitude faced transportation to the colonies in the American South and the West Indies. Jacobites of status sentenced to be forfeited and executed included the insouciant Arthur Elphinstone, sixth Lord Balmerino, the obsequiously repentant William Boyd, fourth Earl of Kilmarnock and, the irredeemably reprobate Simon Fraser, twelfth Lord Lovat. The latter had the unique distinction of a prior conviction for treason in a Scottish court for acquiring his chiefship of the Frasers through abduction, extortion and rape in 1698. Having escaped to join the Jacobite émigrés in France, he was eventually rehabilitated by the Whig establishment for turning informer on the Jacobite cause and then siding with his clan against the rebellion of 1715. During the '45, he had forced his estranged son, Simon, Master of Lovat, to lead out the Frasers to join the Jacobite forces returning from England. Nonetheless, through the assiduous exercise of Scottish political connection at Court, the Master of Lovat was spared further punishment beyond that of forfeiture as was

George MacKenzie, third Earl of Cromarty, who had led the diversionary Jacobite campaign in the northern Highlands. Most Jacobite commanders, including chiefs and leading clan gentry, who survived Culloden were able to escape into exile on the continent where they were to subsist on pensions, military commissions and rents despatched fitfully and clandestinely from their forfeited estates. Ewan Macpherson of Cluny actually hid in a purpose-built cage on Ben Alder in Badenoch, where he ran the first Highland casino for over seven years before joining his former associates, including Prince Charles Edward Stuart, in permanent exile.

Atrocities and legal discrimination markedly slackened off after the Young Pretender escaped to the continent in September 1746. His five months in the heather since Culloden had brought little comfort to the Gael. The Highlanders had not been entirely passive victims, however. A few malevolent government officers, most notably, Munro of Culcairn, were assassinated in Lochaber where the long established cateran tradition of the district was augmented by displaced and harried Jacobite clansmen. Indeed, banditry became the most prevalent form of social protest in the immediate aftermath of the '45 with cateran bands being led by such commissioned and non-commissioned officers as Captain John Roy Stewart and 'Sergeant Mor' Cameron. Conversely, the growth of banditry not only in such traditional haunts as Lochaber and Rannoch Moor, but in most mountainous districts of the southern and central Highlands, enabled government propagandists to press home their aspersions that all Jacobite clans were tainted with banditry and should therefore continue to be subjected to punitive military pressure. The growth of banditry further justified the expansion of the military roads commenced under General George Wade in the 1720s and the erection of a new garrison, Fort George at Arderseir, which was to remain a tangible symbol of the Whig philosophy of progress through repression.

No less enduring was the cultural alienation caused by the repressive conduct of chiefs and leading clan gentry for whom the defeat of Jacobitism at Culloden provided the excuse to throw over the traditional obligations of clanship. Over the previous decade, the Whig grandee and chief of Clan Campbell, Archibald, third Duke of Argyll, had provided the model for the commercial reorientation of estate management at the expense of clanship by introducing competitive bidding to secure leases for townships in Mull, Tiree and Morvern; a process which set the lesser clan gentry who exercised a managerial function as tacksmen against the ordinary clansmen as farmers and labourers. Although he had to dilute this process prior to the '45 as satellite families partial to Jacobitism were out-bidding his own clansmen, he celebrated Culloden by carrying out clearances of the disaffected in Morvern, a procedure soon to be followed by the Duchess of Gordon in Lochaber. Before opting for genocide, Cumberland had actually contemplated transporting all the Jacobite clans from Lochaber and surrounding districts until further enquiries suggested this policy was not cost-effective. Cumberland was actually encouraged to adopt the former option by another Whig chief, Donald Mackay, Lord Reay, who opined that it was easier to conquer than to civilise barbarous people. Commercial tensions between the clan elite and their kinsmen and followers were at the root of the defiance of chiefs manifest during the '45 in the mobilisation of MacKenzies in Easter and Wester Ross, MacLeods and MacDonalds in Skye and Mackintoshes and other members of Clan Chattan in Strathnairn and Badenoch for the Jacobite cause. These chiefs promptly distanced themselves politically from their errant clansmen in the aftermath of Culloden as did the non-combatant chiefs of the Stewarts of Appin, the Chisholms of Strathglass, the MacDonalds of Clanranald and, less successfully, the MacDonalds of Glengarry. Although Ludovic Grant of Strathspey had only sided with the Whig government after Cumberland's forces had crossed the Border in pursuit of the retreating Jacobite army, he actually rounded up and handed over for imprisonment and eventual transportation clansmen in Glenurquhart and Glenmoriston who had gone out for the Jacobite cause.

Such abnegation of the personal authority of chiefship, not the Whig government's legislative offensive, was the prime cause promoting the demise of clanship after Culloden. The legislative offensive of 1747 was essentially a sop to English public opinion that required clanship to be rendered impotent before severity could give way to leniency for a rebellious generation. The abolition of heritable jurisdictions of military tenures were projected as paving the way for the inculcation of civility within Scottish Gaeldom. The institutional abolition of regality courts and the extensive modification of the criminal powers of barony courts did not exterminate the personal authority of the chiefs and leading clan gentry. The abolition of military tenures merely confirmed a practice that had become anachronistic prior to the advent of Jacobitism. Although the Whig establishment within Scotland was prepared to affirm that clanship lacked constitutional warrant, informed opinion realised that the personal authority and obligations on which clanship was based did not depend on heritable jurisdictions or military tenures. Nonetheless, these measures and the associated abolition of the office of Secretary of State for Scotland, were supported by the Whig establishment within Scotland, partly as a gesture of appeasement to rampant Scotophobia but, above all, because of the scale of compensation offered to vested interests headed by the Duke of Argyll. Indeed, through his active collaboration with the legislative offensive, Argyll remained the dominant managerial influence in Scottish politics and was able to control the distribution of around £493,000 to the 146 Scottish nobles and gentry whose heritable jurisdictions were abolished or modified. Almost half a million pounds sterling was thereby apportioned to the political elite that had remained loyal to the British State. This was the largest injection of political capital into Scotland since the Treaty of Union. Argyll, who received the largest sum of £25,000, was also to the fore in raising the political as well as the commercial credit of Scotland, as the prime mover in the British Linen Company, chartered to promote banking as well as textiles and financed by a share issue in which loyalist Whigs were invited to subscribe from July 1746.

Whig as well as Jacobite clans were affected by the associated legislation to disarm and to proscribe such cultural trappings as the wearing of tartan and the playing of bagpipes as a warlike instrument. However, Highland members of the Whig establishment in Scotland continued to promote a tartan identity through portraiture. The lingering persistence of Scotophobia was evident in the exclusion of Scotland from the Militia Act that applied elsewhere in the British Isles from 1757. Nonetheless, the associated decision to raise Highland regiments, primarily for their usefulness as a highly mobile and hardy light infantry in North America during the Seven Years War offered a militarist channel for the resumption of the cultural trappings of clanship. More importantly, given the relatively successful, if expendable, deployment of Highland infantry, the raising of regiments offered an imperial channel for the political rehabilitation of the clan elite – most notably, Simon Fraser, Master of Lovat, who was restored to his forfeited estates in 1774. The sterling service of Highland regiments during the American Revolution provided the ostensible excuse for the restoration of the remaining disinherited chiefs and clan gentry and the winding up of the governmental experiment in the direct management of former Jacobite estates by 1784.

In response to a plethora of improving schemes for civilising the
Highlands from unctuous ideologues and putative place-men, the Whig
government had decided that the forfeited estates of Jacobite chiefs and
gentry were to be annexed inalienably to the Crown in 1752. At the same
time, consumer resistance of clansmen to the forfeiture of their chiefs
and leading gentry had been cowed by a final show trial that led to the
execution of James Stewart of the Glens for his purported role as
accessory to the murder of Colin Campbell of Glenure – the
government factor immortalised as 'the Red Fox' – near Ballachulish
Ferry. Another eight years were to elapse, however, before the
Commission entrusted with the management of the Annexed Estates
became operational. In addition to promoting loyalty to the Hanoverian
dynasty, the Commission was charged to civilise the Gael, diversify the
Highland economy and promote Presbyterianism. The latter task was to
be carried out in association with the Society for the Propagation of
Christian Knowledge in Scotland (whose Gaelic acronym was
appropriately C.C.C.P.). Deficient financing and administrative
indifference ensured that the impressive blueprints to transform the
Highlands commercially and industrially never got off the drawing
board. Primarily the Annexed Estates became an agency for the
relocation of demobilised soldiers and sailors, a task not infrequently

*3. Lochaber No
More by J B
MacDonald.*

*In this highly
romantic painting
Charles Edward
Stuart is shown on
his departure from
Scotland.*

*Dundee Art
Galleries and
Museum*

achieved by the removal of erstwhile clansmen. The Annexed Estates did have a significant exemplary role not so much as a civilising as an accelerating agency for the break-up of traditional townships through the creation of single-tenant farms, planned villages and crofting communities. The consequent removal and relocation of people became an official model for clearance for restored Jacobite as well as loyalist Whig landlords. The lifting of the proscription on tartan in 1782 was small consolation for the Highland casualties of clearance.

Note on Sources

The principal unpublished primary sources consulted were the extensive Loudoun Scottish Collection in the Huntington Library, San Marino, California; the Hardwicke Papers in the British Museum and the Argyll Papers in Inveraray Castle (the latter with the assistance of a Major Research Grant from the British Academy). Among the published primary sources the most significant were *The Lyon in Mourning*, H Paton ed., 3 vols, Scottish History Society, Edinburgh, 1895-6; *A List of Prisoners Concerned in the Rebellion*, W MacLeod ed., Scottish History Society, Edinburgh, 1890; *More Culloden Papers*, vol. 5, D Warrand ed., Inverness, 1930; *The Albemarle Papers, 1746–47*, C S Terry ed., 2 vols, The New Spalding Club, Aberdeen, 1902; *Highland Songs of the Forty-Five*, J L Campbell ed., Scottish Gaelic Texts Society, Edinburgh, 1984; *Scots Magazine*, 1745–7 and *Virginia Gazette of Williamsburg*, 1745–6. The following secondary sources offer contrasting opinions Sir C Petrie, *The Jacobite Movement: The Last Phase, 1716–1807*, London, 1950; B Lenman, *The Jacobite Risings in Britain, 1689–1746*, London, 1980; W A Speck, *The Butcher: The Duke of Cumberland and the Suppression of the '45*, Oxford, 1981; A J Youngson, *The Prince and the Pretender: A Study of the Writing of History*, London, 1985; F J McLynn, *The Jacobites*, London, 1985.

APPENDIX I
A JACOBITE
CHRONOLOGY,
1685-1867

1685   Succession of James VII of Scotland and II of England.

1688   Birth of male heir which would lead to Catholic succession, results in invitation to Protestant William of Orange, with Mary (James's daughter), to rule Britain.

William lands unopposed at Torbay; 'The Glorious Revolution'; James flees to France.

1689   13 February – William and Mary proclaimed joint monarchs of England.

1689   RISING

April – William and Mary proclaimed joint monarchs of Scotland.

John Graham of Claverhouse ('Bonnie' Dundee) raises Highlands for James VII and 11.

27 July – Battle of Killiecrankie. Government forces routed, but Dundee killed.

18 August – Battle of Dunkeld, after which defeated Highlanders disperse.

1690   Building of Fort William, (on site of Monck's Fort at Maryburgh, Inverlochy) to pacify region.

1692   13 February – Massacre of MacDonalds of Glencoe. Highlands subdued after this event.

1701   Death of James VII and II. James Edward Stuart, his son, recognised by the French King Louis XIV as James VIII of Scotland and James III of England ('The Old Pretender'). War of the Spanish Succession begins.

1702   Anne, sister of Mary, succeeds to throne.

1707   Act of Union between England and Scotland.

1708   **REBELLION**

February – Army of 6000 and French fleet assembled at Channel ports for invasion of Britain.

March – fleet sails with James on board but after engagement with Royal Navy in Firth of Forth, coupled with French commanders' lack of commitment to the expedition and bad weather, the attempt fails and the invasion fleet returns to France.

1713   War of the Spanish succession ends with Peace of Utrecht.

1714   Queen Anne dies without heirs and is succeeded by Protestant George, Elector of Hanover, great grandson of James VI and I. He becomes George I, the first of the Hanoverian monarchs.

1715   **REBELLION – 'The '15'**

25 September – James' standard raised at Braemar.

French landings expected in Scotland.

12 November – Battle of Preston.

13 November – Battle of Sherrifmuir. Indecisive result.

22 November – James lands in Scotland near Aberdeen.

1716   4 February – James embarks for France.

Disarming Act passed by the British Parliament.

1717   The regent of France (Duke of Orleans) for infant Louis XV attempts to improve relations with Britain and requests James leave France. The Stuart Court moves to Italy.

1719   **REBELLION**

7 March – James arrives in Spain.

29 March – Main Spanish expedition dispersed by storm.

13 April – Jacobites set up HQ at Eilean Donan Castle on west coast of Scotland.

10 May – Warships fire upon and destroy Eilean Donan Castle.

10 June – Battle of Glenshiel. Spaniards surrender. End of rebellion.

1720   Charles Edward Stuart – 'The Young Pretender' – born.

1720-40 House of Hanover consolidates its position. General Wade builds forts and 238 miles of roads to quell any thoughts of Highland support for more attempts at a Stuart rising and raises Independent Companies of Government Highlanders. Fort William strengthened and further forts built at Inverness (Fort George), Kiliwhimin (later Fort Augustus), Bernera, Ruthven-in-Badenoch and Inversnaid (on Loch Lomondside).

1725	Disarming Act passed by the British Parliament.
1739	The Highland Regiment the 'Black Watch' formed.
1740	War of the Austrian Succession begins.
1743	Battle of Dettingen: Britain under George II defeats French in Germany.

1744 REBELLION

Charles goes to join French invasion fleet at Dunkirk.

Storms wreck fleet before it sails. Expedition abandoned. Charles remains in France.

| 1745 | 11 May – Battle of Fontenoy; French defeat Duke of Cumberland' |

1745 REBELLION - 'The '45'

5 July – Charles sails from France on board the ship *Du Teillay*. Attacked by HMS *Lion*.

23 July – Charles lands at Eriskay (Coilleag a 'Phrionnsa The Prince's Strand) in the Outer Hebrides.

25 July – Charles lands in mainland Scotland at Loch nan Uamh.

1 August – Reward of £30,000 for Charles offered by British Government.

16 August – First action – two companies of the Royal Scots attacked at High Bridge, near Fort William.

19 August – Raising of the standard at Glenfinnan at the head of Loch Sheil.

17 Sept – Enters Edinburgh.

21 Sept – The Battle of Prestonpans. Government army defeated.

19 Oct – Duke of Cumberland arrives in London from Flanders.

1 Nov – Jacobite army leaves Edinburgh for England.

8 Nov – Jacobite army cross the Esk into England.

10-1 5 Nov – Siege of Carlisle.

17 Nov – Charles enters Carlisle.

25 Nov – Marches to Lancaster.

26 Nov – Marches to Preston and halts.

28 Nov – Marches to Wigan.

29 Nov – Marches to Manchester.

1 Dec – Marches to Macclesfield.

2 Dec – Duke of Cumberland at Lichfield.

3 Dec – Charles marches to Leek.

4 Dec – Marches from Ashburne to Derby and halts.

5 Dec – Council of War – resolves to retreat back to Scotland.

6 Dec – BLACK FRIDAY – Retreat of Jacobite Army begins.

18 Dec – Skirmish of Clifton. Cumberland's vanguard defeated by Jacobite rearguard action.

20 Dec – On Charles's 25th birthday the army fords the Esk back into Scotland.

26 Dec – Charles and the Jacobite Army enter Glasgow.

1746   3 Jan – Leave Glasgow.

8 Jan – Stirling capitulates, but Castle holds.

15 Jan – Duke of Cumberland at Edinburgh.

17 Jan – Battle of Falkirk. Government defeated.

6 Feb – Duke of Cumberland at Perth.

18 Feb – Jacobite army enters Inverness.

20 Feb – Inverness Castle surrenders.

25 Feb – Duke of Cumberland at Aberdeen.

March-April – Prince in area of Inverness.

8 April – Duke of Cumberland marches from Aberdeen.

11 April – Duke of Cumberland at Cullen.

14 April – Charles marches to Culloden House. Duke of Cumberland at Nairn.

15 April – Night march by Jacobite Army on Nairn fails to surprise Cumberland on his birthday.

16 April – BATTLE OF CULLODEN

April-September – Hunt for Charles in Scotland.

26 April – Prince sails from Borrodale, Loch nan Uamh and arrives in Benbecula on Harris. Remains in Outer Hebrides until June 27.

28 June – Charles, with Flora MacDonald, sails for Skye.

29 June – Arrives in Skye.

4 July – Embarks for mainland.

5 July – Arrives at Mallaig, and in hiding in the Highlands of Scotland.

5-12 Sept – In 'Cluny's Cage' on Ben Alder.

13 Sept – Leaves for Loch nan Uamh on hearing of French ships.

19 Sept – Reaches Borrodale, Loch nan Uamh and the ships.

20 Sept – *L'Heureux* with Charles on board weighs anchor and sails for France.

Disarming Act passed by British Parliament to proscribe Highland way of life, including dress.

1748   War of the Austrian Succession ends.

1750   Charles visits London and formally converts to Anglicanism.

1752   Jacobite plot to assassinate Royal Family discovered.

1753   Disarming Act of 1746 renewed.

Execution of Archibald Cameron (younger brother of Donald, 'gentle Lochiel'), the last Jacobite to be executed.

1760   Accession of George III.

1766   James VIII and II dies.

1782   Partial repeal of Disarming Act of 1746.

1788   Charles dies.

1807   Death of Charles's brother Henry (IX), Cardinal of York, and the last direct Stuart claimant.

1810   Last military constructed road in Scotland (Perth to Perth Prison).

1817   Last Jacobite arrest.

1820   George III dies; succeeded by George IV.

1824   Patrick Grant 'Auld Dubrach', (b. 1713) a veteran of Culloden dies. He had been introduced to George IV at Holyroodhouse as 'his Majesty's oldest enemy'.

1867   Repeal of the 1746 Disarming Act.

APPENDIX II
Charles Edward Stuart and the British Royal Family

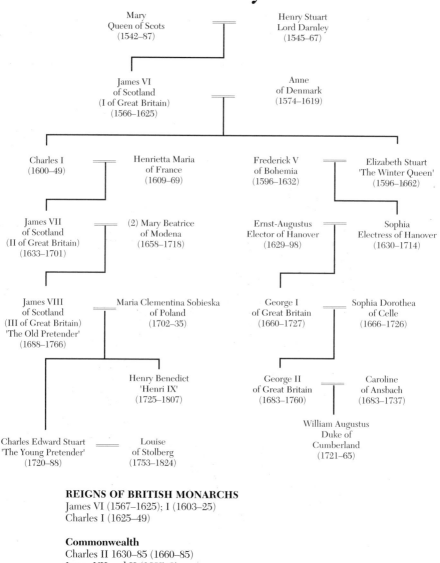

Mary Queen of Scots (1542–87) ═══ Henry Stuart Lord Darnley (1545–67)

James VI of Scotland (I of Great Britain) (1566–1625) ═══ Anne of Denmark (1574–1619)

Charles I (1600–49) ═══ Henrietta Maria of France (1609–69)

Frederick V of Bohemia (1596–1632) ═══ Elizabeth Stuart 'The Winter Queen' (1596–1662)

James VII of Scotland (II of Great Britain) (1633–1701) ═══ (2) Mary Beatrice of Modena (1658–1718)

Ernst-Augustus Elector of Hanover (1629–98) ═══ Sophia Electress of Hanover (1630–1714)

James VIII of Scotland (III of Great Britain) 'The Old Pretender' (1688–1766) ═══ Maria Clementina Sobieska of Poland (1702–35)

George I of Great Britain (1660–1727) ═══ Sophia Dorothea of Celle (1666–1726)

Henry Benedict 'Henri IX' (1725–1807)

George II of Great Britain (1683–1760) ═══ Caroline of Ansbach (1683–1737)

William Augustus Duke of Cumberland (1721–65)

Charles Edward Stuart 'The Young Pretender' (1720–88) ═══ Louise of Stolberg (1753–1824)

REIGNS OF BRITISH MONARCHS
James VI (1567–1625); I (1603–25)
Charles I (1625–49)

Commonwealth
Charles II 1630–85 (1660–85)
James VII and II (1685–9)
William of Orange II (of Scotland);
    III (of England) 1650–1702 (1689–1702) ⎱ Joint monarchy
Mary II 1662–94 (1689–94) ⎰
Anne 1665–1714 (1702–14)
George I (1714–27)
George II (1727–60)

APPENDIX III
MAP:
CHARLES EDWARD
STUART
IN BRITAIN 1745–6

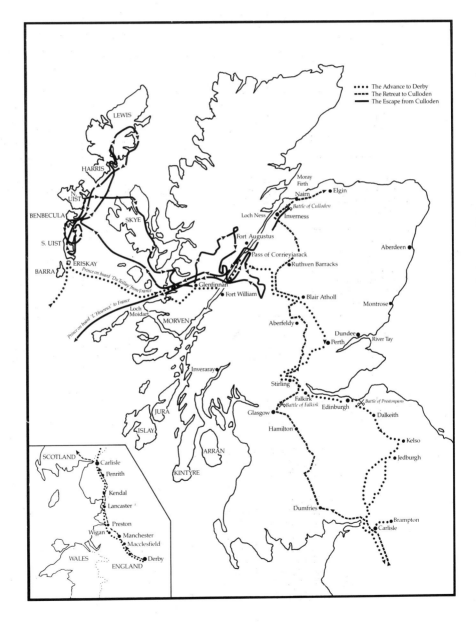

INDEX

Page numbers in italic indicate illustrations

⚜HMSO

HMSO Bookshops
71 Lothian Road, Edinburgh EH3 9AZ
0131-228 4181 Fax 0131-229 2734
49 High Holborn, London WC1V 6HB
(counter service only)
0171-873 0011 Fax 0171-831 1326
68–69 Bull Street, Birmingham B4 6AD
0121-236 9696 Fax 0121-236 9699
33 Wine Street, Bristol BS1 2BQ
0117 9264306 Fax 0117 9294515
9-21 Princess Street, Manchester M60 8AS
0161-834 7201 Fax 0161-833 0634
16 Arthur Street, Belfast BT1 4GD
01232 238451 Fax 01232 235401
The HMSO Oriel Bookshop,
The Friary, Cardiff CF1 4AA
01222 395548 Fax 01222 384347

HMSO publications are available from:

HMSO Publications Centre
(Mail, fax and telephone orders only)
PO Box 276, London SW8 5DT
Telephone orders 0171-873 9090
General enquiries 0171-873 0011
(queuing system in operation for both number
Fax orders 0171-873 8200

HMSO's Accredited Agents
(see Yellow Pages)

and through good booksellers

Printed in Scotland for HMSO by
CCNo 37907 30m 5/95